The Complete Guide
To Grilling Steak

The Complete Guide to

GRILLING STEAK

Master the Cuts, Rubs, and Grilling Techniques

Frank Campanella

ROCKRIDGE
PRESS

Cover Designer: Erin Rinker
Interior Designer: Carlos Esparza
Art Producer: Sue Bischofberger
Editor: Anne Goldberg
Production Editor: Jax Berman
Production Manager: David Zapanta

Photography © Nadine Greeff/Stocksy.com, p. ii; © Andrew Cebulka/Stocksy.com, p. vi; © Jeff Wasserman/Stocksy.com, p. viii; © Maya Visnyei/Offset.com, p. x; © StockFood/Tre Torri, p. 30; © Cameron Whitman/Stocksy.com, p. 58; © Cameron Whitman/Stocksy.com, p. 86; © StockFood/Gräfe & Unzer Verlag/Zanin, Melanie, p. 98.

Illustration used under license from shutterstock.com.

Paperback ISBN: 978-1-63878-198-1
eBook ISBN: 978-1-63878-546-0
R0

To all the great friends and family I've shared a meal with,
to all the late-night barbecue sessions, cooking and
grilling until the sun comes up—memories I will cherish forever.

CONTENTS

≡

INTRODUCTION ix

1: Your Road Map to
Perfect Steak Every Time 1

2: Steak Classics 31

3: Steak Unleashed 59

4: Steak House Sides 87

5: Rubs and Sauces 99

MEASUREMENT CONVERSIONS 108

INDEX 109

Grilled Strip Steak with Charred Tomatoes (page 57)

INTRODUCTION

I have been cooking for as long as I can remember. More specifically, I have been grilling. It started when I was a youngster, flipping burgers and dogs in the backyard at family cookouts. Years later I took my first job as a dishwasher at a local pub. From the dish pit, I watched the grill cooks flip glistening steaks with perfect diamond grill marks as they managed a five-foot grill loaded with steaks of all kinds. I knew that I wanted to work the grill station.

I quickly worked my way up to prep cook and eventually made it to the grill. It was incredibly intimidating to be responsible for cooking hundreds of expensive cuts of beef all to different temperatures. Eventually, I could manage an entire grill, determining the temperatures of each steak just by touch. I became the best grill cook at the restaurant, even though I was only 20 years old. Years later, after I had been a chef at numerous restaurants, I would still jump on the grill just to show the younger cooks that I still had it. In this book, I'm bringing you my years of experience cooking on grills of all kinds to get you started on the road to steak perfection.

Grilling steak presents advantages and disadvantages. Weather will always play a significant role in cooking outdoors, even on gas grills. Learning how to handle these environments and overcome them is half the fun of grilling. Cooking with an open flame is a skill humans have been developing and mastering since we emerged from caves. The fascination with open-fire cooking is nothing new, but we have come a long way in harnessing its power and flavor.

There is a very satisfying feeling when you grill meat perfectly and serve it to the people you care about. (Most of my family enjoys a nice juicy medium-rare steak, but one person does insist on eating their steak well-done. I would call out that family member, but she did give birth to me, and I gladly prepare her steak to her liking.) The information in this book will teach you to cook any cut to a specific temperature with confidence. My goal is to give you the knowledge to feel confident in your ability to grill the perfect steak every time.

In the chapters ahead, we will go over a variety of different methods and discuss what cuts are best for specific preparations. We will also learn what to look for when buying meat and where to shop. Once that foundation is in place, we can begin to build on different sauces, rubs, and side dishes to serve with the steak. We will cover classic steak recipes from around the world, as well as some creative twists on steak house classics that I have served at my restaurants over the years. Whether you are just starting out or have been grilling for years, I have no doubt that you will come away with lots of helpful tips.

After reading this book, my hope is that you will be able to grill steaks of all cuts to perfection, both in flavor and tenderness. Additionally, I want you to be able to manage a fire and prepare steaks using a variety of different methods and types of heat. By the end of this book, you will be a master of cooking over an open fire and be able to grill with the best of them. I encourage you to stay humble after mastering this skill and share your wisdom with others. Remember, with great steak comes great responsibility.

Enough talk. It's time to light up the grill, season those steaks, and get cooking!

Rosemary-Crusted Prime Rib (page 46)

YOUR ROAD MAP TO PERFECT STEAK EVERY TIME

Before we get cooking, let's learn the rules of the grill. In this chapter, I'll cover all the basics and more about different cuts and how to shop for, grill, and serve them. I'll address some age-old questions (to marinate or not to marinate?), explain why you should be friends with your butcher, and discuss the ins and outs of different styles of grills and how to cook with different fuels and types of heat.

UNDERSTANDING STEAK

The more you know about the cut of beef you are going to grill, the better your odds of successfully cooking it. Each cut has its own personality and will handle differently with different methods of cooking and seasoning—high heat versus low heat; smoking versus grilling; seasoning versus marinating. To make sure you get the best results, it's important to educate yourself not just on the cooking process but also on the features of the meat itself. This will inform your choices about how to prepare it.

Tenderness

A good rule to keep in mind is that the leaner the cut of meat, the tougher it will be. Put another way, fat equals tenderness. If you haven't noticed, cows are quite large animals that can weigh the better part of a ton. It takes some powerful muscles to keep that large frame moving around. The cuts that come from these muscles are incredibly tough because of all the connective tissue and muscle fibers. Any cuts of beef from weight-bearing muscles will benefit from low and slow cooking, marinating, or other tenderizing methods. The only exception to this rule is the tenderloin, which is very lean but also incredibly tender since it is not a weight-bearing muscle.

Fatty cuts like the strip loin and rib eye come from areas that are not weight bearing and yield very tender, prized cuts of beef. Eye of round steak is a delicious and affordable cut but can be incredibly tough, so I always recommend cutting it against the grain into slices as thin as possible for optimal tenderness. Sirloin, strip steak, and tri-tip are all cuts that are lean but have enough fat and marbling to become tender when cooked to temperature. These steaks are ideal for hot and fast grilling methods and can be served medium-rare, if desired.

Another factor that influences tenderness is the quality of the meat. We will go into greater detail about the grading system for beef later, but poor-quality steaks tend to be chewier and tougher than higher quality steaks. When it comes to beef, you really do get what you pay for. That said, methods such as marinating, reverse searing, or sous vide cooking can make an inexpensive steak taste like a much more expensive steak.

There is nothing wrong with choosing cheaper cuts of beef as long as you don't skimp on quality. I often say that anybody can make an expensive steak taste good, but it takes some real talent and skill to make an inexpensive cut come out tender. Not all of us, myself included, can afford to be grilling filet mignon every night, but if you shop smart and know what to look for, you can make steak a regular item at the dinner table.

Flavor

Many different factors go into the flavor of beef, including fat content, the diet of the cow, and how the meat was aged. All these variables—including the grade of the cattle—will determine the flavor of the beef as well as the overall mouthfeel.

PERCENTAGE OF FAT

The fat content of a steak influences not just texture but also flavor and mouthfeel. A fatty cut like rib eye or strip steak will have an almost buttery flavor, whereas leaner cuts like sirloin tend to be bolder and more robust. Both are delicious; it really comes down to personal preference and how you choose to cook them. As the meat is grilled, the fat begins to melt and bastes the steak as it cooks. Leaner cuts will dry out more quickly and can become tough and chewy, while a fatty cut will stay juicy even after the steak rests for a few minutes before slicing.

When we talk about the percentage of fat, we are taking into account both the fat that is on the outside of the steak and the marbling of intramuscular fat within the steak. Prime and Wagyu steaks tend to have more marbling and produce a more tender steak when grilled.

How much fat should be on the outside of the steak is more of a personal preference and depends on how much extra trimming you want to do at home. Since beef is normally sold by the pound, the butcher will leave as much fat on as they can to increase the total weight of the steak.

DIET

A lot of people don't realize that the diet of the cow plays a huge part in the flavor of the beef. Meat from pasture-raised cattle, whose diet consists of 100-percent grass and straw, tends to be leaner overall and have a firmer texture than grain-fed cattle. Grass-fed beef does have several nutritional benefits, including a higher ratio of omega-6 to omega-3 fatty acids. On the flip side, the flavor of grass-fed beef tends to be more intense due to its higher mineral content, similar to a dry-aged steak.

Grain-fed cattle makes up about 90 percent of the beef in the United States because it is cheaper to produce. The cattle may still graze in pastures, but the majority of their diet comes from corn. Grain-fed cattle also grow much larger due to their high consumption of carbohydrates from grain and soy. Their meat tends to be slightly sweet and slightly more tender.

My personal favorite is beef from cows that are grass fed but then finished on grain—it's the best of both worlds. These cattle are typically pasture raised and not given any antibiotics or growth hormones. For the last four to six weeks, they are fed a diet of grain and soy to fatten them up so ranchers can get a better price for their cattle. This also gives the beef a better flavor and texture.

AGING

Aging just means letting the meat dry out. This process can be done with large primal cuts or even with smaller individual roasts. Dry aging shrinks the overall weight of the beef, intensifying its flavor. Dry-aged beef is stored uncovered in low-moisture rooms with constant airflow. As the meat begins to lose moisture, the flavor of the beef is intensified. The length of this process can range from as few as seven days to well over 60 days. Dry-aged beef can have an earthy, almost mushroom-like flavor and has a very musty aroma. Dry-aged beef is prized for this flavor, and it tends to be more expensive due to the special care and refrigeration it requires.

Wet-aged beef is butchered and then packaged in plastic and held. Most vacuum-sealed meat you find in grocery stores is technically wet aged for at least a week just in the time it takes to get from the processor to the grocery store. Wet aging is a fairly new practice that involves vacuum sealing individual cuts for up to 10 days in cold rooms with temperatures kept just above freezing. The process does enhance the flavor of the meat; however, the result is much milder than dry aging.

THE STEAK THAT'S RIGHT FOR YOU

It can be daunting to choose the "best" steak when there are so many variables, such as cut, aging, and how the beef was raised.

The best steak for you may not be the best steak for someone else. Some people like leaner cuts like sirloin or tenderloin, while others want a big juicy porterhouse. You may love a bone-in steak and be bored by filet mignon! Even what temperature you like your steak cooked to may differ between cuts due to differences in flavor and texture. I prefer my tenderloin to be cooked to medium, but I like my New York strip medium-rare. You may find you like just the opposite. The beauty of having your own steak is that you can cook it just how you like it.

At the end of the day, you should buy the best steak you can afford. There is no need to take out a second mortgage to buy a steak. Look for deals at big-box stores or buy whole primal cuts and then cut them into individual steaks and freeze them. Try different cuts and—using the resources and recipes in this book—try different grilling methods until you find your holy grail.

BUYING STEAK

Before you light the grill, let's talk about buying steak and what to look for. There are many cuts of steak, and there is a wide range of quality within those same cuts. Many different factors go into determining the tenderness and flavor of a steak. You also need to know the best places to purchase steak and the questions to ask when selecting the right steak for you. Let's discuss these factors a little more in depth and talk about how to purchase the best steak for the money.

Butcher vs. Supermarket

The two most common places to buy steaks are the grocery store and the local butcher shop. You can find great beef at both places, but there are some big differences between the two. Your local butcher shop is most likely a small family-owned business with years of knowledge about the various cuts of beef, including which are best for the recipe you're preparing. That knowledge does come with a price tag. You will find that the average price of beef at a butcher shop is higher than at your local grocery store. This is because butcher shops often purchase their beef from local farms and do all the butchering in-house. Grocery stores mostly use factory-farmed beef that is processed in huge facilities before being sent as individually packaged steaks to the store. The advantage of these large operations is that they can sell beef at a much lower cost than a local butcher shop can. You pay a premium price at a butcher shop, but you also get higher quality, locally raised beef.

If your grocery store does have a butcher counter display case, the meat in it will be fresher than the individually packaged meats found in the coolers. Center-cut steaks will be the most tender and have less connective tissue. End pieces are often tougher and better for well-done steaks that cook longer. When you are shopping in the display case, whether it's at a butcher shop or a grocery store, it's important to chat up the person behind the counter. A good butcher should be passionate and knowledgeable. Every good butcher I've ever met will tell you what the best cuts they have are before you even ask.

TALK TO YOUR BUTCHER

When I shop for a steak, I try to be flexible. If I went there looking for a rib eye but the strip steaks look better and are cheaper, I may change my mind and go with the strip steak. Sometimes I'll just ask my butcher, "What's looking good today, Carl?" Carl will tell me what the best steaks are that day, or he'll tell me about a cut he recently prepared himself. If he doesn't have what I'm looking for, he will gladly custom cut a steak for me. If the butcher isn't helpful or won't go the extra mile for you, that's a sign that you need to look for another butcher. If you need a lot of steaks cut specially for you, try to call ahead. And it's never a bad idea to leave the butcher a tip. I guarantee that will go a long way the next time you stop by.

Meat Quality Grades

The USDA (United States Department of Agriculture) has eight grading levels for beef. The three grades that you will most commonly find are prime, choice, and select. All three of these grades are worthy of the grill but vary in overall quality:

Prime beef is the highest quality. Only 2 percent of beef in the United States is graded to this level. Prime beef is traditionally sold to hotels and restaurants because of its high quality, but in recent years it has become more available in high-end grocery stores and butcher shops. Prime beef comes from a young well-fed cow that has outstanding fat marbling and texture.

Choice is the second-best grade for beef and is also very high quality. It is much more affordable than prime and can be found at most retail stores. The marbling is still very good, but it is not as uniform as prime.

Select beef is the third-best grade, but it still makes for a great steak. This beef may be slightly tougher than a prime or choice cut, but using marinades and solid grilling techniques can turn it into a delicious meal.

Other Labels

Besides the USDA shield displayed on beef packaging, you will see many different labels used by retail stores to further classify the beef. Sometimes these terms are just to entice the customer and have little to no real meaning, while other labels do indicate quality.

Grass fed means that the cow was pasture fed on grass for the majority of its lifespan, but it can still be grain fed before slaughter to bulk up the animal. If you are looking for truly grass-fed beef, look for the term *grass finished*, which means the cow was fed on only grass for its entire life.

Angus beef is a breed of cattle known to be of higher quality than other breeds. Most of the time, only prime and choice grades of beef will be labeled "Angus." The term *Black Angus* refers to this breed's black hair, which is often associated with these high-quality cattle. To be classified as Angus beef, the cow has to have only a small percentage of Angus blood. Certified Angus Beef is a specific brand that prides itself in selling full-blooded Angus beef.

Wagyu and Kobe are specific breeds of Japanese cattle known for their extreme marbling and high fat content, which makes them incredibly tender and expensive. Kobe is a region in Japan where the cattle are often massaged and fed beer or sake to help relax them, which is believed to create the most tender meat. Australia and the United States have begun breeding these same Japanese cows using some of the Japanese breeding methods to create an incredibly high-quality yet more affordable version for consumers. Wagyu is graded on a separate scale that is determined by the marbling of the beef.

Certified organic is a designation that refers to various aspects of the way the beef was raised, including whether its feed was organic. This certification is managed by the USDA and follows a strict protocol throughout the production process.

All natural, on the other hand, is a designation that is not regulated and has little actual meaning. Stick to looking at the grade of the beef or the breed to help you decide what steaks to buy, and don't fall for marketing buzzwords.

What to Look for When You Shop

When shopping for beef, there are some things you can look for to help you purchase the best steaks possible. First off is the color. The steaks should be a beautiful bright red and not have gray or brown shades. If the beef looks gray, it has oxidized, and although it's not harmful, that means it's been on the shelf for a while.

You can also look at the amount of exterior fat. Every steak should have a thin layer of exterior fat but not more than about half an inch. Fat in the marbling within the meat serves the purpose of keeping the meat juicy and tender, but the exterior fat should be trimmed to a thin layer. Otherwise, you are paying for fat that is going to melt away when you cook the steak.

Also, look for clean-cut steaks without any jagged edges or punctures from the butcher. Any steaks with large tears or shredded edges should be avoided.

The last thing to look for is any interconnective tissue that runs through the center of the steak. Avoid steaks that have what looks like a long white streak running through the entire length of the steak because that streak will be very chewy and it is a sign that the steak was an end cut. Always look for uniform center-cut steaks, which will be more tender and have a much better texture and mouthfeel.

STEAK THICKNESS

Steak thickness is a matter of preference, but it also contributes to how the steak will cook. I think 1½ to 2 inches is perfect. That is thick enough that you can develop a perfectly grilled exterior crust without overcooking the center. Don't hesitate to ask the butcher or the person behind the counter to custom cut a steak. You can also call ahead and place your order so the butcher has time to cut your steaks and have them ready when you arrive. I would rather buy one 2-inch-thick steak and serve it family-style than buy three thin steaks.

KNOW YOUR STEAKS

This will be one of the sections you will be able to reference like a cheat sheet every time you're deciding which cut of steak you want to use in a recipe. In this section, we'll go over every major cut of beef and the best ways to prepare them. We'll also discuss the flavor profile and tenderness of each cut so you can decide which steak will work best for you. Beef is so versatile, and each cut has its advantages and disadvantages. Selecting the right steak for the job ensures that your recipe will be executed to perfection.

RIB EYE

Also known as: Cowboy steak, tomahawk, prime rib, Delmonico steak

Source: Located on the top of the cow, above the rib and just behind the chuck

Flavor and tenderness: This cut has outstanding marbling and a higher fat content than other cuts. Rib eye is incredibly tender and juicy with a rich, decadent but balanced flavor.

Best way to prep: Horseradish, rosemary, and Worcestershire sauce are often paired with rib eye. Because of its rich flavor and tenderness, there is no need to marinate. Instead, keep the seasoning simple with salt, pepper, and garlic.

Best way to cook: Though rib eye and prime rib come from the same cut, their preparations are very different. Whole roasts (prime rib) are cooked over low heat for hours, while individual cuts of rib eye can be seared over direct heat. Thick-cut rib eye and tomahawk steaks can be grilled using the reverse sear or sous vide method to ensure the perfect temperature.

FILET MIGNON

Also known as: Beef tenderloin, filet of beef

Source: Located at the top of the loin

Flavor and tenderness: Filet mignon is by far the most tender cut. It is also very lean. The flavor of the tenderloin is milder than that of other cuts due to the lack of marbling.

Best way to prep: Because filet mignon is lean, it benefits greatly from heavy seasoning and the accompaniment of compound butters and rich sauces like hollandaise or béarnaise sauce. The filet will sometimes be encrusted with coarsely ground pepper for a spicy addition.

Best way to cook: Filet mignon can be grilled over high heat or seared in a cast-iron skillet with butter, garlic, and herbs. You can also roast the tenderloin whole and slice it into individual steaks. Filet is best served at no more than medium for optimal juiciness and texture.

T-BONE/PORTERHOUSE

Also known as: No known alias

Source: These steaks are crosscuts of the whole loin, which includes both the tenderloin and the strip loin, separated by the T-bone. The T-bone cut comes from the back of the loin, and the porterhouse from the front.

Flavor and tenderness: Essentially two cuts in one, these steaks have the tenderloin (source of the filet mignon) on one side, which is lean with a mild flavor. The strip loin on the other side has much better marbling and fat, giving you a slightly firmer mouthfeel and bolder beefy flavor.

Best way to prep: These steaks can be seasoned and prepared similarly to the filet and strip steak, though because of the large bone, they will take longer to cook. Season heavily with salt and pepper or your favorite steak seasoning.

Best way to cook: The only difference between a T-bone and a porterhouse is that the T-bone has a smaller filet portion, causing the steak to cook faster on the filet side. Try to grill these cuts with the strip loin side closer to the heat source to protect the filet side from overcooking. I recommend dual-zone grilling. You can carve the filet and strip loin off the bone after grilling and slice each cut, making this a great steak for sharing.

STRIP STEAK

Also known as: New York strip, strip loin

Source: Runs alongside the filet mignon on the loin of the cow

Flavor and tenderness: Overall, this is a very lean cut, but the strip loin has a higher fat content and more marbling than the tenderloin. Strip steaks are the perfect balance of tenderness and fat content, making this one of the most popular cuts of beef.

Best way to prep: Strip steaks are best seasoned with salt and pepper but can benefit from bolder seasonings as well. Because of its rich flavor, there is no need to marinate this cut. Much like the tenderloin, strip steaks also benefit from a peppercorn crust, which adds texture and flavor.

Best way to cook: Grill the strip steak over medium heat with the bone removed or with the blade bone attached. Boneless strip steaks will cook slightly faster, so keep an eye on the internal temperature. Strip loins are best served medium or rarer.

TOP SIRLOIN

Also known as: Sirloin steak, beef tips

Source: Cut from the top loin above the strip loin

Flavor and tenderness: Top sirloin is a lean cut often served family-style as a large steak that's great for slicing against the grain. It's a very affordable cut with a firmer texture than a strip loin. Top sirloin will have intramuscular connective tissue that can be chewy.

Best way to prep: This cut is a good candidate for marinating with Worcestershire sauce, garlic, and herbs or soy sauce and cilantro. You may also want to tenderize the sirloin to break up any connective tissue.

Best way to cook: This steak is best served medium or medium-rare. I avoid cooking this cut rare because it can be chewy. You can grill this cut whole over direct heat or slice it into thin medallions and sear for just a few minutes per side over high heat.

FLANK STEAK

Also known as: Vacio, bavette

Source: Lower abdomen on the undercarriage toward the back quarter

Flavor and tenderness: Flank steak is incredibly flavorful and has an optimal balance of fat to lean meat. However, this cut can be a bit tough, so it's a steak that you will want to slice.

Best way to prep: Flank steaks are great for marinating with many different flavors. You can use Southwestern flavor profiles or Mediterranean flavors to help tenderize this cut.

Best way to cook: Flank steak is best grilled over high heat as a whole steak until medium or medium-rare then served thinly sliced against the grain. This cut can also be butterflied open, stuffed with fillings, and rolled back up and sliced into pinwheels.

SKIRT STEAK

Also known as: Fajita meat, inside skirt, outside skirt

Source: Located in front of the flank steak, attached to the diaphragm muscle

Flavor and tenderness: Skirt steak is a boneless cut that comes in long strips that can be cut into smaller sections. Like flank steak, skirt steak can be tough if not sliced thinly against the grain. The flavor is bold and lends itself to many different cuisines, but in the United States it is commonly used in Southwestern and Mexican preparations like fajitas and tacos.

Best way to prep: Skirt steak may require a little bit of trimming, but most of the fat will melt away when grilled. This cut can also be shredded for many different recipes. You can season it with many different flavors—jerk seasoning and fajita blends are two of my favorites. Skirt steaks are also prime candidates for marinating to tenderize and incorporate different flavor profiles.

BOTTOM SIRLOIN

Also known as: Bottom sirloin butt, ball tip steaks, petite sirloin

Source: Behind the loin on the lower end of the sirloin

Flavor and tenderness: This cut has a rich, bold flavor like flank or bavette steaks, but it is much less expensive. Bottom sirloin is firm in texture and should be thinly sliced when served.

Best way to prep: Thinly slicing or cubing for stew is a great way to use this cut. If grilling it as a steak, be sure to marinate and tenderize it to break down muscle fibers.

Best way to cook: This cut is best grilled over high heat to medium or medium-rare. Always slice thinly against the grain and serve with sauces or beef stock to help keep it juicy.

HANGER STEAK

Also known as: Hanging tenderloin, butcher's steak

Source: Located just below the rib on the plate section, located in the sternum near the belly

Flavor and tenderness: This steak is tender and firm at the same time due to its ratio of fat to lean meat. Classically, this cut has been reserved by butchers for their own consumption because it's so flavorful.

Best way to prep: Hanger steak is very flavorful, so it can be seasoned simply with salt and pepper or your favorite steak seasoning. This cut requires very little trimming and can be cooked as is.

Best way to cook: Hot and fast is the best way to grill a hanger steak. It can be served on salads or sandwiches because of how tender and juicy it is. When served as an entrée, hanger steak is often sliced against the grain and served with light accent sauces or compound butter.

DENVER STEAK

Also known as: Chuck steak

Source: Cut from the chuck, located on the front shoulder above the brisket

Flavor and tenderness: Denver steaks have a wonderful balance of tender lean meat and rich, buttery marbling, which separates this steak from other cuts. This cut is a tender steak but can be slightly chewy, so it's best served sliced against the grain. Though similar to a sirloin steak, the Denver cut is trimmed into lean strips, making it great for grilling like a strip steak.

Best way to prep: Denver steaks are great when marinated and can be seasoned in several ways, from garlic and herbs to Southwestern or South American flavors. To make this steak even more tender, you can use a Jaccard tenderizer to perforate any connective tissue and help break down muscle fibers when cooking.

Best way to cook: This cut is best served medium or medium-rare because it tends to dry out when overcooked due to its lower fat content. The most popular way to prepare this cut is to grill it over direct heat, searing the meat to create a charred crust. It's great for slicing for tacos and topping salads.

FLAT IRON

Also known as: Blade steak

Source: Comes from the sternum or belly on the front shoulder

Flavor and tenderness: The flat iron steak is the second-most tender steak (the most tender is the filet mignon) with more flavor and marbling than a tenderloin. This cut is often overlooked at steak houses but is one of my personal favorites due to its affordable price and bold flavor.

Best way to prep: Flat iron doesn't require much prep and can be seasoned very simply with salt and pepper or your favorite steak seasoning. Most of the time, flat iron steaks require zero trimming and can go straight from the package to the grill.

Best way to cook: Flat iron steaks are usually no more than one inch thick, so hot and fast grilling is your best bet. This cut is best served no more than medium and can be sliced to share or served as an individual cut.

ROUND STEAK

Also known as: Eye round steak, rump steak, wafer steak

Source: Comes from the backside of the cow, just above the shank located on the rump

Flavor and tenderness: This cut looks like a filet mignon because of its very lean marbling yet is much tougher than the filet. These steaks have a robust beefy flavor but will dry out quickly due to their low fat content.

Best way to prep: Round steaks are one of the tougher steaks you will find and should be marinated for at least 24 hours and tenderized using a Jaccard tenderizer to help break down their muscle fibers. Using acidic juices like pineapple in the marinade can help with tenderness.

Best way to cook: Grill hot and fast over direct heat to medium-rare. This cut needs moisture and fats added to keep the steak from drying out. Serve with sauces or beef au jus to keep the steaks hydrated.

SHORT RIBS

Also known as: Korean short ribs, flanken-cut short ribs, plate ribs

Source: Found next to the brisket or chuck on the cow's belly or undercarriage

Flavor and tenderness: Flanken-cut short ribs are crosscut into ¾-inch-thick strips so they can be grilled quickly and still come out tender. Because the meat is thin, marinade can penetrate deep into the beef, and the beef will retain all the flavor of the marinade. This also helps tenderize the short ribs. High-heat preparation caramelizes the outside of the short ribs to intensify the flavors used in the marinade.

Best way to prep: Flanken-cut short ribs benefit from marinating overnight using ingredients like citrus, garlic, and soy sauce, which also help tenderize the meat. Whole short ribs tend to be seasoned with salt and pepper or barbecue dry rubs to complement the flavor of this cut.

Best way to cook: Korean-style short ribs are crosscut into thin strips, about ½ inch thick, and are marinated for hours so they can be grilled quickly over high heat.

TRI-TIP

Also known as: Bottom sirloin roast, triangle steak

Source: This cut comes from the bottom of the sirloin roast on the loin of the cow

Flavor and tenderness: Tri-tip is an incredibly flavorful cut with very robust flavors. The texture is lean and tender, but it can be chewy if not sliced correctly.

Best way to prep: Tri-tip is the perfect cut for marinating, traditionally with Southwestern chiles and spices. Tri-tip is best cooked whole. You can marinate it for up to 48 hours.

Best way to cook: Tri-tip will range in size from 1½ to 3½ pounds, and it has an unusual boomerang or triangle shape with grains that run in two directions. Cut the roast in half at the point of the triangle and then slice each piece against the grain.

Tri-tip is often grilled over wood or charcoal at high heat to develop a crust then moved to indirect heat to finish cooking. You can also use the reverse sear or sous vide method to cook tri-tip. Most of the time, tri-tip is served medium or medium-rare, but some people prefer to smoke tri-tip like a brisket and cook it low and slow to about 200°F.

FIRING UP THE GRILL

Once you have selected the perfect steak and brought it home, it's time to light the fire and start grilling. The method of grilling needed to cook the perfect steak will vary depending on the thickness of the steak and the cut you've chosen. Thinner steaks will be grilled hot and fast over direct heat. Bigger, thicker cuts will need to be grilled using dual-zone or indirect grilling methods. Let's go over both methods and discuss the advantages of each.

Direct Fire

This is the most simple and straightforward method of grilling. The steak is grilled on high heat directly over the heat source and turned every few minutes until it is cooked to your desired internal temperature. This method is best for thinner steaks or for people who like very rare "blue" or Pittsburgh-style steaks.

CHARCOAL GRILL

If you are using direct heat with a charcoal grill, you need to build an even bed of charcoal so that the temperature is consistent under the entire surface area of the grill. You can use a charcoal chimney to light the charcoal, or you can use a blowtorch to light the coals. To build the fire, remove the grill grate and pile up coals in the center of the grill. Be sure you have enough charcoal to cover the entire area of the grill. For a kettle-style grill, I normally use two chimneys worth, or about five pounds of charcoal.

Once all the coals are lit and starting to glow, use a raking tool or tongs to spread them out into an even layer. At this point, I like to add a few more briquettes scattered about the grill so the fire will burn longer. Once the coals are spread out, put the grill grate and lid back on. Make sure the bottom damper is about three-quarters open and the top damper is about halfway open. It should take 5 to 10 minutes for your grill to reach 550°F to 600°F. If the grill is having trouble reaching temperature, open the top damper all the way. The vast majority of charcoal grills have a built-in thermometer on the lid, but if yours doesn't, you can use a probe thermometer that clips to the grill grates to monitor ambient temperature. If all else fails, use the old-school method: Hold your palm just above the rim of the grill where the grate will sit. If you can't hold it there for more than three to four seconds, you've reached sear temperature.

When the correct temperature is reached, remove the lid and use a brush to clean the grill grates. Then brush the grates with a few paper towels dipped in vegetable oil—this will make sure the steak doesn't stick and will also help you achieve those perfect grill marks. The whole process of lighting up the charcoal grill and getting it up to temperature should take 20 to 30 minutes.

GAS GRILL

A gas grill is much easier to light and bring up to temperature since you simply have to turn the knob and make sure the burner ignites. Gas grills vary in size, the number of burners, and BTUs, so get acquainted with your grill's specific dials and temperatures. Before you light the grill, check the propane tank. There is nothing worse than running out of propane mid-grill, and you'll likely overcook or undercook the steaks while changing out tanks.

Always make sure all the burners are clean so the flame can burn evenly. If the burners are dirty, the grill will either not burn hot enough or have hot spots in different areas, which can lead to uneven grilling.

Once you have checked the fuel and made sure the burners are clean, it's time to light the grill. Every gas grill is different, so read the instruction manual before using your grill. Once all burners are lit, turn the dials to about 50 percent power and shut the lid. It should take around 10 minutes for the grill to reach 550°F to 600°F. If the grill hasn't reached temperature within 10 minutes, turn the dials up to 75 percent power or higher if needed.

After the grill has come to temperature, brush off the grill grates the same way you would a charcoal grill and brush the grates with oil to prevent sticking. If you have a larger grill with four or more burners, you can turn one burner off to keep as a resting area for the steaks while still maintaining an ideal grilling temperature.

THE EISENHOWER STEAK

This steak preparation method is named after the 34th president of the United States, Dwight D. Eisenhower, as it was his preferred way to eat steak. In this preparation, a thick cut of steak is placed directly on the coals, giving the meat a charred, crispy exterior with a rare to medium-rare center. Use hardwood lump charcoal instead of briquettes for better flavor. (Hardwood will also burn hotter.) Season the steak with only salt; do not add oil, which could cause flare-ups when cooking. Unfortunately, this method can't really be achieved using a gas grill, so this is only for my charcoal grillers.

To prepare the Eisenhower steak, simply build a hot bed of coals and place the steak directly on the coals once they are searing hot. You will hear the steak sizzle immediately, but once it's on the coals, don't touch it for three to four minutes to create a charred crust. The steak will take somewhere around 12 minutes for medium-rare. You can use any cut of beef you like, but it needs to be at least 2 inches thick. This method is most often used with bone-in rib eye steaks, porterhouse steaks, or T-bone steaks because they're thick and the bone makes it easier to pick the steak up out of the fire. You'll want to either have a long pair of metal tongs or fireproof gloves to rotate the steak.

When rotating the steak, you may notice little pieces of charcoal stuck to the meat. Simply brush them off back into the grill and continue cooking. Once the steak is cooked to your liking, let it rest for about five minutes before slicing.

A steak prepared this way may also be called char steak, campfire steak, or coal-fire steak.

Indirect Fire

Indirect or dual-zone grilling is a method in which half of the grill is set up for high-heat direct grilling and another zone is set for roasting at a lower temperature. The advantage to this method is that you can sear the steak over direct flame and then move it to the indirect zone to slowly bring the meat up to the ideal internal temperature without burning it.

Indirect grilling is best for thick-cut and well-done steaks that take longer to cook.

CHARCOAL GRILL

Less charcoal is required for dual-zone cooking than for direct grilling since you only need a coal bed for half of the grill. You can use a chimney or fire starters just as you would with direct grilling, but make sure all the coals are spread evenly only on the one side. After all the coals are burning hot and you have spread them out evenly on one side, scatter a few more unlit coals over top before placing the grill grates in the grill. You should have two "zones"—one directly over the coals and one over the half with no coals.

Make sure the bottom damper is about three-quarters open and the top damper is open about halfway. If you have a kettle grill, build your fire so the coals are on the same side as the lid damper. Let the grill temperature come up to 550°F to 600°F, opening the top damper more if needed. Because you have fewer coals, you may need to open the dampers all the way to reach the ideal grilling temperature. This will also cause the coals to burn faster, so make sure everything's ready by the time you reach grilling temperature, or you'll risk the grill cooling off before you've finished cooking. As with all grills, I recommend wiping down the grill grates with a paper towel dipped in oil before you start to cook, to clean them and prevent the meat from sticking.

GAS GRILL

For dual-zone grilling using a gas grill, simply divide your grill into two zones depending on how many burners you have. If your grill has an even number of burners, turn half of them up to high and leave the other half on the lowest setting. If you have an odd number of burners, turn one side up to high, the middle burner to 50 percent, and the other side to its lowest setting. Clean the grill grates with a brush and then brush on a light coating of oil before grilling.

Achieving Sear Temperature

There is a reason we sear steaks over an open fire instead of boiling or baking them. That seared crust, which can only be achieved by intense high heat, gives steak the classic flavor that makes it a favorite eating experience of so many. That robust flavor is all thanks to the Maillard reaction. When amino acids and sugars reduce, it creates a caramelization on foods of all kinds, but it is especially noticeable on meats. Whenever you see the golden crust on grilled cheese, pan-seared dumplings, or grilled meats, you know the flavor and texture will be superior.

Achieving the perfect sear is something we all strive for. Restaurants use ovens and grills that can reach well above 1,000°F to sear their meats. Your grill may not reach temperatures that high, but if you leave the meat on a hot, well-seasoned grill just a little longer, you'll have a beautifully seared steak every time. One of the most common grilling mistakes is when someone places their meat on the grill and then moves it within a few seconds. In these cases, the meat often sticks and ends up with a gray exterior that is less than appetizing. Once that meat hits the grill, *leave it alone*! Give the Maillard reaction time to take place.

The initial sear is the most important stage of the grilling process. I know it can be scary when you see the flames flaring up, but resist that urge to pick up the steak and move it. Let the steak sear for at least a minute. Look for the crust to begin developing on the underside of the steak, then slide the edge of the tongs or spatula underneath the steak and lift it just enough to check the underside for that char-grilled crust before flipping it.

Another method that has become increasingly popular is the reverse-sear method, where you slowly bring up the temperature of the steak over low heat, cooking indirectly, then sear the steak just long enough to create a crust on both sides. This method allows you to monitor the temperature of the steak, especially a large, thick-cut steak, and sear it for just a few minutes to finish.

YOUR GRILL TOOLBOX

To be successful at anything in life, you need to have the right tools for the job, and grilling is no different. Here is a list of utensils and other items to make your grilling experience a safe and delicious one. If you don't have everything on this list, that's okay; over time you can add these helpful tools to your collection.

* **Instant-read thermometer:** This is the single most important tool when it comes to grilling, especially for beginners. More experienced cooks can use different methods to judge the internal temperature of meats, but the most precise method is using an instant-read thermometer.

* **Ambient temperature (probe) thermometer:** Most gas and charcoal grills now have a thermometer attached to the lid of the grill, but having a probe attached to the grill grates themselves will give you a much more accurate measurement of the grilling surface and can substitute for a built-in thermometer if you own one of the few grills that don't come equipped with one.

* **Cutting board:** A good cutting board is the best surface for cutting meats. You can use wood or plastic boards, but find one that is at least ½ inch thick.

* **Fire extinguisher:** Safety first, as they say. Hopefully you never need to use a fire extinguisher, but if you are cooking with an open flame, it's a good idea to have one around.

* **Chimney starter:** If you are using a charcoal grill, you will need a way to get your charcoal lit. Chimney starters are great because you can simply light up the bottom with some newspaper and have bright red coals in about 10 minutes.

* **Spring-loaded tongs:** Find a pair of tongs that have a good weight and a firm spring. There is nothing worse than going to pick up a steak and dropping it on the ground!

* **Sharp chef's knife:** When slicing a steak, you want to have a good, sharp knife. A dull knife will tear the steak or cut unevenly.

* **Spray bottle:** You may get the occasional flare-up when grilling. Spritzing a little water can knock down the flames to prevent the meat from burning.

* **Heat-resistant gloves:** These are great for picking up large roasts or moving meats around the grill. Gloves can also be helpful if you have a flare-up or want to protect your arms and wrists when using tongs.

PREPPING THE STEAK

A great-quality steak doesn't need more than seasoning and a hot grill, but other steaks may need a little more attention to help elevate their flavor and tenderness. Whether you should leave a steak alone or marinate it really depends on the marbling and the cut of steak. Rib eye, filet mignon, and strip steaks rarely need more than a healthy dose of salt and pepper. Other cuts, like sirloin or round steaks, benefit greatly from marinating and tenderizing before grilling to help break down their muscle fibers. The right technique for the right steak can make the difference between a great meal and a mediocre one.

Before seasoning, it's important to examine the steak for any imperfections the butcher might have overlooked. Look for sharp bone fragments or any discolorations that should be removed. Sometimes the steak may have more fat on the outside than you prefer and can be trimmed down. Trimming excess fat can also prevent flare-ups while gilling. The majority of steaks won't require much trimming, but it's always good to give the steak a once-over before grilling so every bite is as delicious as the last.

The Importance of Salt Brining

Salt is the most important ingredient when it comes to steak, as it brings out incredible amounts of flavor. Dry brining is the process of seasoning the steak before you cook it— the salt melts into the meat and also brings out moisture, which will cause the steak to firm up. After dry brining, be sure to pat the steak dry and remove any excess moisture before searing. For dry brining, kosher salt or a large-crystal salt is preferred. Table or granular salt dissolves too quickly and is easy to overuse when seasoning. Kosher salt is the perfect size and is hard to overseason with. Dry brine should be applied to the steak about 30 minutes before grilling. I don't recommend dry brining longer than an hour or two unless you're preparing a large roast.

Other Seasonings

Besides salt, there are a variety of seasonings that can be used on steaks and roasts. While purists will tell you that a good steak needs nothing more than a pinch of salt, others will season their steaks with elaborate blends of herbs and spices. Cajun seasoning, jerk, and barbecue rubs are often applied to cuts of meat that will be cooked longer to achieve a more tender piece of meat. These seasonings can really enhance leaner pieces of meat that don't have as much fat and can elevate their flavors tremendously.

These steak seasonings are low in sugar, which is a hazard since it can burn and get bitter. (Also, avoid leafy herbs, which can burn when grilling.) Here are some of my favorite spices for steak.

- **Coriander:** This is the seed that the cilantro plant comes from. Coriander has a slightly nutty flavor, especially when roasted, as well as hints of citrus and floral notes.

- **Cumin:** This spice adds a smoky, earthy flavor that is used in a variety of Mexican and South American recipes.

- **Paprika:** Most often ground, paprika comes in different varieties, including smoked, Hungarian, and sweet. Avoid using this spice in excess because it can burn when exposed to high heat.

- **Granulated onion:** Use granulated onion instead of onion powder, which can clump and taste bitter. Granulated onion adds a slightly sweet flavor to beef.

- **Granulated garlic:** Like granulated onion, granulated garlic is a better choice than garlic powder, which can clump. If you love garlic, this seasoning is a must.

- **Black pepper:** Other than salt, freshly ground black pepper is probably the most common seasoning used on steak. If you use pre-ground pepper, use a coarse grind rather than a table grind.

- **Rosemary:** This is one of the few herbs I recommend using with steak because of its sturdy, woody needles. Rosemary adds a unique herbaceous flavor.

Marinades

Now that we've discussed all the different ways to season a steak, let's shift gears and talk about marinades and when to use them. Marinating can transform chewy, tough cuts into tender, moist, delicious steaks and roasts. Cuts like round steaks, London broil, and skirt steak are all great for marinating. Marinating food involves submerging it in a seasoned liquid that often contains acidic elements like vinegars or citrus juices. Marinades not only impart flavor but also tenderize meats by dissolving tough connective tissue and muscle fibers. Marinating too long, though, can turn certain cuts mushy and discolored, so it's important to use the right marinade for the right cut of meat.

You might start with a very simple marinade of salt, pepper, lemon juice, olive oil, and garlic to give the meat an extra punch of flavor. Simple marinades like this can be used on just about any cut of steak and need only a few hours to impart flavor. Before grilling, it's important to remove any excess marinade and pat the meat dry with a paper towel. You can then season the steak and grill it without worrying about flare-ups.

DO MARINADES TENDERIZE MEAT?

Certain ingredients in marinades and brines contain enzymes that can tenderize meats. Bromelain, for instance, is an enzyme found in pineapple, papaya, and some other tropical fruits that are used in a variety of meat tenderizers in both liquid and powder form. The enzyme works by breaking down proteins into smaller proteins and digesting them. Other ingredients like citrus or vinegar can tenderize meat, but if left on too long, they will turn the meat discolored and mushy. Oil-based marinades can be used overnight or even for a few days, while citrus and vinegar marinades need only 30 minutes to an hour to tenderize meat. Thick, tough cuts can benefit greatly from these tenderizing enzymes to break down chewy steaks and turn them into tender, delicious beef.

Using marinades to tenderize meat is nothing new. Marinades have been used in different cooking methods around the world for thousands of years. Bulgogi is a thinly sliced Korean beef dish that is marinated with Asian pear or pineapple, turning tough cuts of beef into amazingly tender strips that are then seared, making the meat almost fork-tender. Skirt and flank steak are marinated with vinegar and lime juice to tenderize the meat for tacos and fajitas. Marinade used with sliced meat can often be cooked as a sauce with the meat, but for thick cuts, the excess marinade should be removed from the steak to achieve a better crust.

Injections

On some larger cuts like London broil, flank steaks, or tri-tip, you can use a meat injector to puncture the meat and inject brines and marinades directly into it. This added flavor can speed up the marinating process from hours to mere minutes. Meat injectors can be found at most hardware stores in the grilling section, or you can purchase them online. The needle is large enough to use any brine or marinade you like, as long as it doesn't have any large chunks of herbs or spices that might clog it up. You can inject the meat 15 minutes before grilling, and you can really tell the difference in flavor as well as tenderness. Another advantage of injecting the meat is that you can inject the marinade inside but dry brine the outside with salt, giving you the best of both worlds.

Using a Jaccard or Meat Mallet

The Jaccard meat tenderizer is one of my favorite gadgets to tenderize tough cuts of meat and allow marinade to penetrate thick cuts of beef. A Jaccard is a tool that has several rows of two-sided sharp blades that make hundreds of small holes in all sorts of meats. These punctures break down tough connective tissue and allow brines and marinades to work their way deeper into the meat in shorter amounts of time.

Most Jaccards have springs in them, so as you press down on the tenderizer, the spring will retract so as not to tear the meat. To use the Jaccard, simply press the blades down onto the meat, much like pressing a stamp onto an envelope. You can tenderize an entire piece of meat or use it only on the areas with connective tissue.

A meat mallet will also tenderize tough cuts, but it tears and flattens the meat, so it's normally only used on thin cuts of meat that you want to cook quickly. Since both tools will tenderize meats but the mallet will damage the steak, I don't recommend using a meat mallet for beef unless you're making thin cutlets.

STEAK ON THE GRILL

In this section, we'll go over the process of cooking steak, including tips to make sure it comes out perfectly every time. We will discuss different methods and situations so you can decide which is best for the specific steak you are grilling. Because everyone likes their steak cooked differently, it's important to know how to prepare a beautifully charred Pittsburgh-style steak as well as a well-done steak that doesn't taste like it's been vaporized (it can be done). Grilling steak should be a fun, relaxing experience, not stressful. Being able to grill great steaks is a skill you'll have for as long as you cook, and I think it is a life skill everyone should have, whether you grill frequently or just a few times a year.

Blot It Dry

We touched on this earlier, but I can't stress enough how important it is to blot steaks dry before grilling them. Moisture on the outside of the steak will cause the meat to steam instead of sear. Even if you dry brined and seasoned the steak, you should still blot it dry and re-season it just before it hits the grill. Whether you are searing a steak in a cast-iron skillet or grilling it over direct flames, you always want to keep excess moisture to a minimum.

If you marinate the steak, wipe the steak on the rim of the container, reserving the marinade, then pat it dry with some paper towels. Season the steak with the same dry spices that were in the marinade so you can maintain the flavor profile without the marinade steaming the meat. Once you have a good sear, you can baste the steak with that excess marinade to impart more flavor to the meat.

ROOM TEMP OR STRAIGHT FROM THE REFRIGERATOR?

Here is a slightly controversial take on a subject often argued over when it comes to grilling. Should you pull the steak out of the refrigerator and bring it up to room temperature before cooking, or can you grill it cold, straight from the refrigerator? I've literally grilled thousands of steaks, and I very rarely have time to let a steak sit on my counter to come up to room temperature. Grilling a cold steak is better, especially if you are grilling a thin steak and you want to get a good crust without overcooking it. If you want to pull the steaks out while you are lighting the grill, that's fine, but I doubt that the temperature of the steak will rise significantly in the 15 to 20 minutes it takes to prepare the grill for cooking.

For Thick Steaks

When grilling a thick-cut steak, you may need to move the steak off of direct heat so it can finish cooking without burning. In these cases, I almost always set up the grill for dual-zone cooking. Start by searing the steak for two to three minutes per side over direct heat. Once you have developed a good crust, check the internal temperature of the steak using a probe thermometer; chances are the steak still isn't cooked to your desired temperature. Move the steak over to the indirect zone and continue to cook until you have reached the desired internal temperature. This method can be done on both a charcoal and gas grill. When you are searing a steak over direct heat, leave the grill open to fuel the fire with oxygen and to keep an eye on the steak to avoid flare-ups. Once you move the steak to indirect heat, put the lid on to maintain the temperature of the grill as the steak finishes cooking. This method is great for cooking medium, medium-well, and well-done steaks without burning them.

Although the temperature of the grill will go down as you sear the steaks with the lid open, you will still have plenty of heat to develop a deep crust. Once you have seared the steak and moved it to indirect heat, the grill will recover slowly to ideal roasting temperatures. You can set up the grill the same whether you are using a charcoal or gas grill. On a charcoal grill, move your coals to one side of the grill and leave the other side empty. On a gas grill, turn on half of the burners and leave the other half of the burners off, or set at their lowest setting, to create an indirect zone.

ON SEARS, REVERSE SEARS, FLARE-UPS, AND CHARGRILLED FLAVOR

Even though we focus on grilling steaks in this book, there are many other ways to cook steak that may not involve the grill at all. There are also methods such as reverse searing or sous vide that don't start on the grill but finish there. Sometimes it's fun to explore new cooking methods to see what you like best.

* **Reverse sear:** Instead of searing the steak first, you can season the steak and cook it in the oven or in a smoker over low heat. Make sure you have a probe thermometer in the steak so you can monitor the temperature. You can then sear the steak for just a few minutes per side to finish it off.

* **Sous vide:** This is similar to the reverse-sear method, but the steak is placed in a vacuum-sealed bag and then placed into a container of warm water that is temperature-controlled using an immersion circulator. You can control the specific temperature of the water, and the steak will never overcook once it reaches its set temperature. To finish the steak, you just remove it from the bag, pat it dry, season, and then sear to finish. This method does require additional equipment; you will need to have an immersion circulator and a vacuum sealer for best results.

* **Pan searing:** This method is often used for steak that you intend to serve with a sauce, because once the steak is cooked, you can remove it to rest while you prepare a quick pan sauce like you would for steak Diane or steak au poivre. The steak will develop a beautiful caramelized crust while retaining a juicy center.

* **Butter basting:** When the steak has almost finished cooking, you can finish it by placing a knob of butter in a hot cast-iron skillet with a sprig of rosemary or thyme and a few cloves of garlic. Once the butter begins to turn golden, place the steak in the pan and begin spooning the foaming brown butter over the steak for about 30 seconds to infuse the crust of the steak with the roasted herb and garlic flavor.

* **Finishing salts:** Most every steak is seasoned with kosher salt, but finishing salts are coarse and flaky salts that are sprinkled on top of the steak just before serving. Finishing salt adds a burst of flavor as well as a crunchy texture to the tender steak. Maldon or Celtic salt are two popular types of finishing salts.

For Thinner Steaks

Thin steaks should be grilled over direct heat because of their short cook time. I recommend making sure the steak is as cold as possible because you'll have more time to develop a crust on it without overcooking it. It's important to have all the seasonings, cooking utensils, and everything else you need ready to go, because once the steaks hit the grill, you need to pay attention. Instant-read thermometers won't help you here because it's hard to get an accurate temperature on thin steaks. Instead, look at the crust, and depending on your desired internal temperature, you will be able to judge how long to cook the steak. The longer you cook the steak, the darker the outer crust will be. A rare steak will have a lighter shade crust and feel softer than a well-done steak, which will have a dark, almost charred color and be very firm. Medium-well and well-done are no problem because overcooking isn't really an issue. Rare and medium-rare steaks require more precision, because you have to cook them just long enough to get grill marks on the steak and they are done within five minutes, depending on their thickness. Just like thick-cut steaks, you can grill thin steaks on both charcoal and gas grills using the exact same method. Keep the lid off the grill the entire time to make sure you don't overcook the steaks.

Getting to Done

When grilling a steak, one of the most important factors is simply cooking it to your desired temperature. Whether you like your steak well-done or rare, you need to use proper grilling techniques to make sure your steak comes out perfectly every time. We will go over everything you need to know to grill steaks to the correct doneness no matter how thick or thin the steak is.

LEVEL OF DONENESS

Everyone has their own opinion about how done a steak should be. Some people are leery of a red or pink interior and prefer a well-done piece of meat. The longer you cook the steak, the less moisture the steak will have. For me, the perfect steak is cooked medium-rare, and this tends to be the most popular internal temperature for steak. You will find that most chefs recommend their steaks cooked no more than medium because they believe that any further cooking will degrade the quality and flavor of the beef. That said, if you prefer your steak medium-well or even well-done, you should have it the way you want it. Just be aware that it will take longer; a well-done steak won't be ready in 10 minutes.

The amount of time it takes to grill a steak will depend on the steak's thickness and the temperature of the grill. Knowing this, we can estimate that you will sear each steak for two to three minutes per side, and then depending on how you prefer your steak, you'll need to continue cooking until you hit your desired internal temperature. Each level of doneness will have less red color as it cooks until you reach well-done, where you will find no red or pink left in the center.

For example, a rare steak that's about $1\frac{1}{2}$ inches thick will take seven to nine minutes to cook to an internal temperature of 120°F. The steak will be cool in the center with a bright red color.

A medium-rare steak will be done in 10 to 12 minutes and should read between 120°F and 130°F. The center will be slightly less red and warm in the middle.

Medium steaks will take 13 to 15 minutes and will be in the 130°F to 140°F range. You will find a warm pink center, but it will still be very juicy.

Medium-well steaks should take somewhere between 17 to 20 minutes and be cooked to 140°F to 150°F. A steak cooked to this temperature will have traces of pink, be slightly juicy, and have a hot center.

A well-done steak will take the longest, somewhere in the range of 20 to 25 minutes, to cook to an internal temperature above 160°F. There should be no pink left in a well-done steak. It will be gray in color and have a very hot, dry center.

BLACK-AND-BLUE

A black-and-blue steak, also known as Pittsburgh-style, is a steak that's prepared so that the outside is charred to the point where it's almost burned but the center is cold and "blue." Black-and-blue steaks are easier to prepare at restaurants because of the incredibly powerful grills they have. To prepare black-and-blue steaks at home, you will need a carbon-steel pan or an aluminum sizzle platter—these pans are very thin and conduct heat well. Get your grill as hot as it can go, then place the steak on the pan on the grill and shut the lid. Wait two minutes, then flip and cook for another two minutes, then remove immediately. Slice the steak immediately to stop the cooking process. This method only works on thick-cut steaks of two inches or greater. Thin steaks will overcook before a crust develops.

HOW TO CHECK FOR DONENESS

The best way to ensure a perfectly cooked steak is to use an instant-read thermometer. Digital thermometers are much more accurate than traditional analog stem thermometers and rarely need to be recalibrated. When you probe the steak, make sure to take the temperature at the thickest part of the meat, aiming for the tip of the probe to land in the center of the meat. On thin cuts, it can be tough to use a digital thermometer, so you will need to go with look and feel. A rare steak will have a lot of give and feel soft to the touch, whereas a well-done steak will be firm and have almost no give at all.

When to Take It Off the Grill

Let's talk about when to take the steak off the grill. Should you let it rest? Should you slice it right away? Will the steak overcook if you don't eat it right away? Let's jump in—carryover cooking is when the steak continues to cook even after it has been removed from the heat. Carryover cooking is less of a problem on thick-cut steaks that are cooked rare because the internal temperature just isn't that hot. However, on a thin-cut steak, the meat can continue cooking 5°F to 7°F higher after removing it from the grill. The hotter the internal temperature of the steak, the larger the range of carryover cooking.

To combat this issue, remove the steak a few degrees short of the target internal temperature. For example, if you want to cook a medium steak to an internal temperature of 135°F, you should pull it off to rest at around 130°F.

Resting the steak lets the juices in the meat redistribute so that when you slice into the steak, all the moisture doesn't run out onto the cutting board. Think about a pot of boiling water with all the bubbles bouncing around in the pot. If you remove the pot from the water, the boiling slows and the bubbles eventually stop. The same process is happening on a micro level inside the steak. Giving the steak just five minutes to rest will make a big difference in the flavor and juiciness of the steak.

One of the first things I was ever taught about grilling a steak is you can always cook a steak longer, but you can't cook it less. Once your steak is overcooked, there's no fixing it. However, if your steak is slightly undercooked, you can simply put it back on the grill for a few more minutes and cook the steak to your liking. Pro tip: Anytime you are grilling steaks, leave the grill on until you have served the steaks. If any of the steaks need to be cooked longer, you won't have to go through the hassle of relighting the grill. Just be sure that once you've got the thumbs up from your guests, that you do remember to shut the grill down.

Slice It Right

Your steaks have been cooked to perfection and rested. The final step is to slice them up and serve them. You always want to make sure that you are slicing against the grain of the steak. Each cut of beef has a grain, or lines that head in one direction. Slicing across the grain will make each bite easier to chew and create a much better eating experience.

Whether you prefer thick or thin slices, cutting against the grain will increase the tenderness of the steak. Thinly slicing a tougher cut like a sirloin will help make it more tender, whereas a strip steak or a filet mignon can be cut thicker and still be tender. Also be sure to have a sharp knife when slicing beef. You can use a chef's knife or a carving knife but make sure it's not dull, or you may get uneven slices or even tear the meat.

ABOUT THE RECIPES

Now let's get into my favorite part of the book: the recipes. I have put together a collection of recipes for any and all occasions. We start off with classic steak recipes from around the world. These recipes have been adapted for the grill so you can prepare all these dishes outside without losing the heart of the recipes. Restaurant favorites like Steak au Poivre (page 34) and Grilled Steak Oscar (page 44), which are normally cooked in a pan, have been modified for grilling. You will also see internationally inspired steak preparations like Korean Kalbi (page 32),

Thai Beef Salad (page 50), and Picanha with Chimichurri (page 54).

In the Steak Unleashed chapter (page 59), we get creative with some steak recipes that I've prepared throughout my restaurant career. These dishes are truly showstoppers, and I know you're going to love each of these amazing steaks. Some of my personal favorites like Jalapeño-Popper Pinwheels (page 78) and Steak Chesapeake (page 60) have been adapted for home cooks with easy-to-follow instructions so you'll feel like I'm cooking right alongside you. I even added a few nostalgic dishes from my childhood like Salisbury Steak (page 42) and Country Fried Steak with Black Pepper Gravy (page 82) that are so much better than the TV dinner versions I grew up with.

In each recipe, you'll also see a **Steak Swap** tip with suggestions you can use to switch out different cuts of meat if you want to change things up. Each recipe will have a specific steak recommended, but you can substitute other cuts. I'll also give you my **Perfect Partner** recommendations on a side dish I think goes best with each steak. Finally, you'll also see a **Variation Tip** to give you everything you need to grill with confidence and prepare amazing steak dinners that are sure to impress.

Steak Fajitas

2

STEAK CLASSICS

Nobody can lay claim to being the first to grill steak; it's a tradition as old as time and something that is done all around the world. Each culture has different methods and ingredients to enhance the flavor of their steaks. Here you will find a selection of my favorite steak recipes from all around the world. Some are classic French preparations that I have modified to be made on the grill. Other recipes are meant to be cooked over an open flame and require little to no modification. Each of these recipes has a fond place in my heart. They are my favorite way to travel to far-off places without leaving my backyard.

Korean Kalbi 32

Steak au Poivre 34

Steak Marsala 36

Steak Fajitas 38

Eisenhower Cowboy Rib Eye 40

Salisbury Steak 42

Grilled Steak Oscar 44

Rosemary-Crusted Prime Rib 46

Bistecca Fiorentina 48

Thai Beef Salad 50

Blue Cheese and Bacon Carpetbagger 51

South African Braai-Spiced Steak 52

Picanha with Chimichurri 54

Bavette with Burgundy Sauce 56

Grilled Strip Steak with Charred Tomatoes 57

KOREAN KALBI

Serves 4   Prep time: 15 minutes, plus 2 hours or overnight to marinate   Cook time: 35 minutes

Kalbi is a sweet and salty marinated short rib that is grilled over high heat until tender and basted with the reserved marinade until the sauce becomes sticky and the short ribs are a deep mahogany color. The style of short ribs used for this recipe is often labeled "Korean-style" or "flanken." This is because the ribs are crosscut into thin ¼-inch strips that can be grilled quickly, unlike whole short ribs that need to be braised for hours over low heat. This is the cut of short ribs you will usually find at a Korean barbecue restaurant where the meat is cooked tableside.

2 pounds Korean-style short ribs
¼ cup scallions, both white and green parts, for garnish
1 tablespoon sesame seeds, for garnish

For the marinade

1½ cups packed brown sugar
½ cup pineapple juice
⅓ cup soy sauce

3 tablespoons rice wine vinegar
2 tablespoons chili paste, such as sambal oelek
2 tablespoons minced garlic
1 tablespoon minced ginger
1 tablespoon sesame oil
¼ cup water

1. **To make the marinade:** In a large bowl, combine the brown sugar, pineapple juice, soy sauce, vinegar, chili paste, garlic, ginger, and sesame oil with ½ cup of water and whisk until the sugar has dissolved. Add the short ribs to the bowl and make sure they are fully submerged. Cover with plastic wrap and refrigerate for at least 2 hours or as long as overnight.

2. Remove the short ribs from the marinade, making sure to shake off as much of the liquid as possible, and place them on a paper towel–lined plate to absorb any excess marinade.

3. Pour the remaining marinade into a small saucepan and simmer over medium-low heat for 10 to 15 minutes, or until the sauce is thick enough to coat the back of a spoon. Set aside.

4. Prepare the grill for dual-zone cooking with the coals off to one side. Aim for a grill temperature of 450°F to 500°F.

5. Grill the short ribs over direct heat for about 4 minutes per side, closing the lid after each turn, until they develop a deep mahogany color. Move the short ribs to indirect heat and baste with some of the reserved marinade. Turn the ribs and baste the other side, then continue to baste and turn every 3 to 4 minutes, cooking until the sauce becomes sticky and the short ribs have reached an internal temperature of 170°F, 10 to 12 minutes.

6. Transfer to a serving plate and garnish with the scallions and sesame seeds.

★ Steak Swap: This recipe is best prepared with Korean-style short ribs, but if you have to substitute them with another cut, use London broil cut into 2-inch strips.

Perfect Partner: Serve this recipe with white rice and your favorite veggies like Grilled Lemon-Pepper Broccoli (page 95).

Variation Tip: If you can't find chili paste, you can substitute sriracha in this recipe.

STEAK AU POIVRE

Serves 4   Prep time: 10 minutes   Cook time: 25 minutes

When it comes to classic steak house dishes, steak au poivre has to be at the top of the list. This French dish of pepper-crusted steak topped with creamy sauce originated in Normandy in the late 19th century and is often thought of as the original date-night steak because it's typically shared. Steak Diane is a very similar preparation but with the addition of mushrooms to the sauce. Traditionally, this recipe is pan-seared, but I've modified it for the grill, giving you the perfect dish to make for an elevated dinner at home.

For the sauce

3 tablespoons unsalted butter, divided

1 tablespoon minced garlic

1 tablespoon minced shallot

2 ounces cognac

¼ cup beef stock

1 cup heavy (whipping) cream

1 tablespoon chopped fresh parsley

1 teaspoon freshly ground black pepper

½ teaspoon dried thyme

Kosher salt

2 (16-ounce) strip steaks

1 tablespoon avocado oil

1 teaspoon kosher salt

2 tablespoons freshly ground black pepper

1. **To make the sauce:** In a small saucepan, melt 1 tablespoon of butter over medium heat. Add the garlic and shallot and sauté for about 2 minutes, until softened. Add the cognac and beef stock and cook for 3 to 5 minutes, until reduced by half.

2. Add the heavy cream and cook for about 14 minutes, until reduced by half and thick enough to coat the back of a spoon.

3. Remove the pan from the heat and whisk in the remaining 2 tablespoons of butter, the parsley, pepper, and thyme. Season with salt to taste, cover, and set aside to keep warm while you grill the steaks.

4. Prepare the grill for direct-heat grilling, aiming for a grill temperature of around 450°F.

5. Brush the steaks with the avocado oil and then season with the salt and pepper.

6. Sear the steaks for 4 to 6 minutes per side for medium-rare, shutting the lid on the grill in between turns. Once the steaks have reached your desired internal temperature, or 125°F for medium-rare, remove them from the grill and let them rest for 5 minutes.

7. To serve, slice each steak against the grain into ¼-inch-thick slices. Spoon the sauce over the steaks and serve.

★ Steak Swap: Filet mignon or hanger steak would make a great substitution if you can't get your hands on a strip steak.

Perfect Partner: Rosemary-Truffle Fries (page 93) are my go-to side dish with steak au poivre because dipping the fries in the sauce is life changing.

Variation Tip: If you prefer a cast-iron sear of the peppercorn crust, you can prepare the steak following the same instructions. Just place the skillet on the grill over direct heat and sear the outside of the steak to pick up a little grilled flavor.

STEAK MARSALA

Serves 2   Prep time: 10 minutes   Cook time: 30 minutes

Marsala wine is a slightly sweet, fortified wine named after its birthplace in Sicily, where this recipe originated as a way of using this local product. Used to deglaze the pan after sautéing mushrooms, garlic, and fresh herbs in butter, the wine gracefully marries all the flavors. You will find that this velvety sauce pairs perfectly with the richness of the beef.

For the sauce

1 tablespoon diced shallot

1 tablespoon minced garlic

4 tablespoons (½ stick) unsalted butter, divided

1 cup sliced mushrooms

1 rosemary sprig

1 thyme sprig

½ cup marsala wine

½ cup beef stock

Kosher salt

Freshly ground black pepper

2 (8-ounce) hanger steaks

1 tablespoon olive oil

½ teaspoon kosher salt

½ teaspoon freshly ground black pepper

1. Prepare the grill for direct-heat grilling, aiming for a grill temperature of 450°F to 550°F.

2. **To make the sauce:** In a large skillet over medium heat, sauté the shallot and garlic in 1 tablespoon of butter for about 2 minutes, until slightly softened. Then add the mushrooms and continue to cook for 4 to 5 minutes, until softened.

3. Once the mushrooms are tender, add the sprigs of rosemary and thyme and cook for 1 minute, then pour in the wine and beef stock.

4. Simmer the sauce over medium-low heat for 10 to 15 minutes, until the sauce has been reduced by half. Remove the fresh herbs and take the pan off of the heat. Whisk in the remaining 3 tablespoons of butter. Season with salt and pepper to taste. Set aside.

5. Once the grill is hot, brush the steaks with the olive oil on all sides, then season with the salt and pepper.

6. Sear the steaks for 4 to 5 minutes per side, shutting the lid on the grill in between turns. The steaks should take 8 to 10 minutes to reach medium-rare depending on their thickness. Once the steaks have reached your desired internal temperature, or 125°F for medium-rare, remove them from the grill and let them rest for 5 minutes.

7. To serve, slice each steak against the grain into ¼-inch-thick slices. Fan the steak slices out on a serving dish and spoon the marsala sauce over top.

★ Steak Swap: You can substitute any 1- to 1½-inch-thick boneless steak you prefer, from a strip steak or filet to a Denver or flank steak.

Perfect Partner: Marsala sauce goes great with any potato dish, especially roasted Garlic-Herb Hasselback Potatoes (page 89).

Variation Tip: If you don't have fresh herbs, use a ¼ teaspoon each of dried thyme and rosemary in place of the fresh sprigs.

STEAK FAJITAS

Serves 4   Prep time: 10 minutes, plus 1 hour or overnight to marinate   Cook time: 20 minutes

This is the perfect steak recipe for feeding a large group. Fajitas were first served in the 1930s to ranch workers in Texas. Originally fajitas consisted of "lesser" cuts of meat that would have been otherwise thrown away, but over time the dish gained popularity and better cuts like skirt and flank steak were used. Fajitas became a signature of many Tex-Mex restaurants for their enticing sizzling sounds and intoxicating aroma of sautéed meats and veggies served with flour tortillas.

1 tablespoon chili powder

1 tablespoon smoked paprika

2 teaspoons granulated onion

2 teaspoons granulated garlic

2 teaspoons dried oregano

1 teaspoon ground cayenne pepper

1 teaspoon kosher salt

1 teaspoon freshly ground black pepper

½ teaspoon ground cumin

---

2 pounds skirt steak

3 tablespoons avocado oil, divided

2 red bell peppers, seeded and cut into large sections

2 onions, sliced into ¼-inch rings

2 cups whole button mushrooms

8 (8-inch) flour tortillas

For serving

Guacamole

Sour cream

Salsa

Shredded cheese

Refried beans

Romaine lettuce, shredded

Lime wedges

1. In a small bowl, combine the chili powder, smoked paprika, granulated onion, granulated garlic, oregano, cayenne, salt, pepper, and cumin. Set aside.

2. Trim any excess pieces of fat or stringy pieces from the skirt steak, then place it in a resealable plastic bag along with 2 tablespoons of avocado oil and the fajita seasoning. Massage the seasoning into the steak so that the beef is fully coated. Refrigerate for at least 1 hour or as long as overnight.

3. Prepare the grill for direct-heat grilling, aiming for a grill temperature of 400°F to 500°F.

4. Place the peppers, onions, and mushrooms on a platter and brush with the remaining 1 tablespoon of avocado oil. Grill the vegetables for 3 to 5 minutes per side, until they are tender and have a char on the outside. You may need to move the veggies around if there are flare-ups. Once the veggies have a good char on them, remove them from the grill and set aside on a platter.

5. Remove the skirt steak from the marinade and pat it dry with a paper towel.

6. Sear the steak for about 4 minutes per side for medium, shutting the lid on the grill in between turns. Once the steak has reached your desired internal temperature, or 135°F for medium, remove it from the grill and let it rest for 5 minutes.

7. Slice the mushrooms and peppers into slices and separate the onion rings. Slice the steak into 5-inch sections, then cut the sections across the grain into $1/2$-inch strips. Serve the fajitas family-style with the tortillas and your favorite condiments.

★ Steak Swap: **Flank steak would be the closest cut to skirt steak.**

Perfect Partner: **Jalapeño-Cheddar Mashed Potatoes (page 91) are a great side dish you might not think of serving with fajitas, but the flavors work extremely well together.**

Variation Tip: **The beauty of fajitas is that they can be customized. You can make this recipe low carb by serving the fajitas over a salad instead of with tortillas.**

EISENHOWER COWBOY RIB EYE

Serves 2   Prep time: 5 minutes, plus 15 minutes to dry brine   Cook time: 20 minutes

So-called because Dwight Eisenhower reportedly liked his steak cooked this way, this steak is the ultimate Neanderthal-style steak because you cook it directly on the coals. Simply seasoned and cooked quickly, Eisenhower steaks are perfect for larger cuts and are ideal for sharing. If you want to enjoy beef in one of its purest forms, this is definitely a recipe to try. Make sure to use hardwood lump charcoal because it burns hotter, and briquettes leave too much dust on the steak.

1 (1½-pound) bone-in rib eye

3 teaspoons kosher salt

For the cowboy butter

8 tablespoons (1 stick) unsalted butter, at room temperature

2 tablespoons Dijon mustard

2 tablespoons Worcestershire sauce

3 garlic cloves, minced

½ teaspoon red pepper flakes

½ teaspoon freshly ground black pepper

1 tablespoon freshly squeezed lemon juice

2 teaspoons hot sauce

2 teaspoons chopped fresh chives

½ teaspoon chopped fresh thyme

1. Prepare the grill for direct-heat grilling, aiming for a grill temperature of 550°F to 600°F.

2. Season the steak liberally on all sides with the salt. Let the steak sit for about 15 minutes, then pat it dry before grabbing it by the bone and placing it directly on the coals.

3. Sear the steak for 7 to 10 minutes per side for medium-rare. Use tongs or fire-safe gloves to turn the steak and remove any pieces of coal that stick to it.

4. **To make the cowboy butter:** While the steak is in the fire, in a small bowl, combine the butter, Dijon mustard, Worcestershire sauce, garlic, red pepper flakes, pepper, lemon juice, hot sauce, chives, and thyme using a spatula.

5. Once the steak is charred on both sides, check the temperature of the steak, which should be around 125°F for medium-rare. If the steak needs to cook more, push the coals off to one side, then wrap the steak in aluminum foil and place it in the grill beside the fire to continue cooking.

6. Once the steak has reached your desired internal temperature, remove it from the foil and let it rest for about 5 minutes.

7. To serve, slice the steak against the grain into ¼-inch-thick slices and serve with the cowboy butter on the side for dipping.

★ Steak Swap: Substitute a thick-cut porterhouse or T-bone in place of the rib eye.

Perfect Partner: I love to serve Eisenhower steaks with Creamed Spinach (page 88) to add creamy richness to the simply charred steak.

Variation Tip: The key to making this sauce is to not melt the butter but make sure it's completely softened. If the butter melts, the fat will separate, making the sauce greasy.

SALISBURY STEAK

Serves 4   Prep time: 8 minutes, plus 30 minutes to marinate   Cook time: 45 minutes

When I think of classic TV dinners, I think of Salisbury steak, a nostalgic meal that brings me back to my childhood. I've modified the traditional recipe for thin steaks smothered in mushroom gravy so that it's perfect for grilling, making this classic budget meal a grown-up comfort food everyone will love. Salisbury steak was created by Dr. James Salisbury in 1897 as part of a meat-based diet, but the dish didn't reach its height of popularity until the 1960s and 1970s, when the first TV dinners were introduced. Salisbury steak is based on the German recipe for hamburger steak, made from ground beef and served with brown gravy.

1½ pounds round steak or cube steak

2 large onions, sliced crosswise into ¼-inch rings

2 cups button mushrooms

1 tablespoon Worcestershire sauce

1 teaspoon kosher salt

1 teaspoon freshly ground black pepper

For the gravy

4 tablespoons (½ stick) unsalted butter

4 tablespoons all-purpose flour

3 cups beef stock

1 tablespoon dried minced onions or ¼ cup diced white onion

1 tablespoon soy sauce

1 tablespoon Worcestershire sauce

2 teaspoons freshly ground black pepper

½ cup heavy (whipping) cream

1. Prepare the grill for dual-zone cooking with the coals off to one side. Aim for a grill temperature of 400°F to 500°F.

2. In a medium container with a lid, combine the steaks, onions, and mushrooms with the Worcestershire sauce, salt, and pepper. Let sit, covered, for 30 minutes in the refrigerator.

3. **To make the gravy:** While the steak and veggies are marinating, in a large skillet placed on the grill over direct heat, melt the butter and flour together, whisking constantly for about 2 minutes. Add the beef stock, onions, soy sauce, Worcestershire sauce, and pepper and cook, whisking frequently, for about 5 minutes, until the gravy has thickened. Whisk in the heavy cream, then move to indirect heat to keep warm.

4. Remove the whole mushrooms and onion slices from the marinade, place them on the grill, and cook, turning occasionally, until they start to soften, about 6 minutes. Cut the cooked mushrooms into bite-size pieces and add them to the gravy along with the onion rings.

5. Pat the steaks dry with a paper towel and sear for 5 to 7 minutes per side for medium-well. Once the steaks have reached the desired internal temperature, or 150°F for medium-well, remove them from the grill.

6. Submerge the steaks in the gravy and let simmer over medium-low heat for 8 to 10 minutes before serving to allow the steaks to absorb the flavor of the gravy. You may need to move the pan back to direct heat to reach a simmer depending on the grill temperature.

7. Place the steaks on a plate, top with the gravy, and serve.

★ Steak Swap: **For a budget-friendly version of Salisbury steak, you can form ground beef patties into long, round steak shapes and grill just as you would a steak.**

Perfect Partner: **Grilled Lemon-Pepper Broccoli (page 95) and mashed potatoes make great companions for Salisbury steak.**

Variation Tip: **To make the steaks even more tender, you can use a Jaccard tenderizer or meat mallet to flatten out the steaks and tenderize them.**

GRILLED STEAK OSCAR

Serves 2   Prep time: 10 minutes   Cook time: 20 minutes

When you see a steak prepared Oscar-style at a restaurant or steak house, it typically means that the steak is topped with crabmeat and either hollandaise or béarnaise sauce with asparagus on the side. The dish was originally made with pan-seared veal cutlets, but over time it has become more commonly made with steak. This may seem like a strange combination, but I assure you the flavors come together exquisitely. Because of the richness of the sauce along with the crab and the asparagus, you don't need to serve a large portion of steak for this recipe. A 4- to 6-ounce steak will be plenty, so you can splurge on the crabmeat. This is a fun, decadent meal for a special occasion for two.

10 asparagus spears

2 (4- to 6-ounce) flat iron steaks

1 tablespoon avocado oil

1 teaspoon kosher salt

1 teaspoon freshly ground
    black pepper

6 ounces jumbo lump crabmeat

1 tablespoon unsalted butter

For the béarnaise sauce

4 large egg yolks

2 tablespoons freshly squeezed
    lemon juice

1 teaspoon Tabasco sauce

¾ cup (1½ sticks) unsalted
    butter, melted

1 teaspoon white vinegar

½ teaspoon dried tarragon

1. To prepare the steaks and asparagus, trim about 2 inches off the woody ends of the asparagus, brush the steaks and asparagus with the avocado oil, season with the salt and pepper, and set aside.

2. **To make the béarnaise sauce:** Place the egg yolks, lemon juice, and Tabasco sauce in a blender or food processor. Blend for about 30 seconds, until the color of the yolks lightens. Then begin slowly drizzling in the melted butter until the sauce becomes an off-white or pale yellow color, about 60 to 90 seconds. Add in the vinegar and tarragon and pulse to combine. If the sauce is too thick, add a few tablespoons of cold water, 1 tablespoon at a time. Set aside.

3. Prepare the grill for direct-heat grilling, aiming for a grill temperature of 450°F to 500°F.

4. Sear the steaks for 4 to 5 minutes per side for medium-rare, shutting the lid on the grill in between turns. Once you have flipped the steaks and they are halfway done, or around 100°F, in a small skillet or oven-safe dish on the grill, combine the crabmeat and 1 tablespoon of butter and cook just until the butter has melted and the crabmeat is warm, about 2 minutes. While the crabmeat is cooking, place the asparagus spears on the grill and cook for about 4 minutes, until slightly tender but not mushy or limp.

5. For medium-rare, the steaks should take 8 to 11 minutes total, depending on the thickness of the steaks. Once they have reached your desired internal temperature, or 125°F for medium-rare, remove them from the grill and let them rest for 5 minutes.

6. To serve, lay 5 spears of asparagus on each plate, then top with the flat iron steak. Top the steak with the crabmeat and a few dollops of béarnaise sauce.

★ Steak Swap: **Hanger steak or filet mignon would be the best swaps for this recipe.**

Perfect Partner: **Since a vegetable is already included in this recipe, serve this dish with potatoes. Try Garlic-Herb Hasselback Potatoes (page 89).**

Variation Tip: **Once you prepare the béarnaise sauce, store it in a thermos or insulated mug to keep the sauce warm without breaking it.**

ROSEMARY-CRUSTED PRIME RIB

Serves 4 to 6   Prep time: 10 minutes   Cook time: 2 hours

This is the ultimate showstopper when it comes to grilled beef. Bone-in prime rib roast can seem a little intimidating because it's a large, expensive piece of meat, but in all honesty, you cook it just like you would any other steak. It just takes longer because you cook it at a low temperature to avoid burning the herbs. I highly recommend using a probe thermometer with a digital readout so you can monitor the roast's internal temperature without opening the lid.

1 (4- to 5-pound) bone-in
   prime rib roast
¼ cup Dijon mustard
3 garlic cloves, minced

2 tablespoons kosher salt
1 tablespoon freshly ground
   black pepper

2 teaspoons chopped
   fresh rosemary
1 pound cipollini onions, peeled
1 tablespoon avocado oil

1. Prepare the grill for indirect cooking. Because this will be a longer cook, you will use the slow-burn method. Pour out a bed of unlit charcoal in a semicircle around the outside edge of the grill and light only one end of the coals using a blowtorch or by placing hot coals on top of the unlit coals. This will extend the cooking time and keep the temperature in the 300°F to 350°F range.

2. Brush the rib roast on all sides with the Dijon mustard, then season with the garlic, salt, pepper, and rosemary.

3. Place the roast in a cast-iron skillet or roasting pan. Toss the onions with the avocado oil and spread them out in the pan around the roast.

4. Insert a thermometer probe into the thickest part of the roast, then set the roast on the grill as far away from the coals as possible. Make sure that the thicker side of the roast faces the heat source.

5. Cover and cook the roast to about 5°F less than your desired temperature, or about 120°F for medium-rare. Keep an eye on the onions. When they are fully cooked, remove them and set aside while the roast finishes cooking. For medium-rare, it should take about 2 hours to cook, depending on the size of the roast, but monitor the internal temperature throughout the cooking process.

6. Once the roast has reached your desired internal temperature, or about 125°F for medium-rare, remove it from the grill and let it rest for 10 to 15 minutes.

7. To carve, hold the ribs with the bones pointing up. Carve around the bones to remove them all as one piece. Then set the roast flat on a cutting board and slice it into thin or thick slices depending on how many people you are serving. Serve with the onions on the side.

★ Steak Swap: **If you can't find a bone-in roast, a boneless rib roast or a loin roast will also work.**

Perfect Partner: I love to serve this rib roast with my Prosciutto-Wrapped Brussels Sprouts (page 90).

Variation Tip: **Believe it or not, mayonnaise is a fantastic binder and can impart a lot of rich flavors into the crust. If you don't like Dijon mustard, give mayonnaise a try in its place.**

BISTECCA FIORENTINA

Serves 2 to 4   Prep time: 5 minutes   Cook time: 45 minutes

This is one of my favorite steaks to serve to a small dinner party of three or four guests. This giant thick-cut porterhouse is seasoned simply with salt and then brushed with olive oil throughout the cooking process. Bistecca alla Fiorentina is the premiere Italian steak house cut and is quite impressive on the plate. The strip and filet are removed and sliced before returning the cut steak back to the bone to serve. Bistecca Fiorentina steak originally came from a Tuscan breed of cattle known for its incredibly tender meat, which was prized throughout the region. Today, the recipe can be prepared with any variety of porterhouse.

1 (2½- to 3-pound) porterhouse steak, about 3 inches thick
1 tablespoon kosher salt

3 garlic cloves, smashed
1 teaspoon red pepper flakes
¼ cup olive oil

3 rosemary sprigs, tied together with butcher's twine

1. Prepare the grill for dual-zone cooking with the coals off to one side to do a reverse sear. Aim for a grill temperature of around 300°F.

2. Season the porterhouse on all sides with the salt, then place it on the indirect side of the grill.

3. Slowly cook the steak to about 15°F less than your desired temperature, or about 110°F for medium-rare, then remove the steak from the grill and heat up the coals, with the lid off, to around 500°F.

4. As the grill heats up, in a small dish, combine the garlic cloves, red pepper flakes, and olive oil. You will use the bundle of rosemary sprigs as a brush for basting the steak.

5. Once the grill is ready to sear, place the steak over direct heat and sear for about 2 minutes. Once there is a crust on one side, flip the steak over and begin basting with the olive oil mixture using the rosemary brush. Continue turning the steak once every minute, basting each side each time until the steak reaches your desired internal temperature, or 125°F for medium-rare, about 10 minutes, depending on the thickness of the steak. Remove the steak from the grill and let it rest for 5 minutes.

6. To serve, carve off the strip and the filet, then slice each steak against the grain into $3/4$-inch-thick slices. Place the bone on a serving platter or cutting board and reassemble the sliced meat in place. Brush with the olive oil mixture and serve family-style.

★ Steak Swap: **You really should try to find a good-quality porterhouse for this recipe, but the method itself can be used with a tomahawk rib eye or a thick-cut T-bone steak.**

Perfect Partner: **Creamed Spinach (page 88) is a great side dish that can also double as a sauce with this impressive porterhouse.**

Variation Tip: **To get a better crust, you can use the Eisenhower steak method (see page 16) and cook the steak directly in the coals.**

THAI BEEF SALAD

Serves 2   Prep time: 15 minutes   Cook time: 25 minutes

If you are looking for a bright, fresh, herbaceous salad, then you will love this Thai beef salad. It is a great lunch or weeknight dinner recipe, especially in the spring and summer when you are looking for lighter options. I can't get enough of the fresh herbs combined with the lime and fish sauce, a distinctive combination found in Thai cooking. Every bite is bursting with flavor.

2 (8-ounce) hanger steaks
1 teaspoon kosher salt
¼ cup avocado oil
Juice and zest of 2 limes
½ cup lightly packed
   fresh cilantro

1 jalapeño pepper, seeded and
   roughly chopped
3 garlic cloves, chopped
1 (1-inch) piece fresh ginger,
   peeled and chopped
2 tablespoons fish sauce
8 to 10 fresh mint leaves

1 tablespoon honey
1 seedless cucumber, diced
½ cup thinly sliced red onions
1 cup cherry tomatoes, halved
4 cups lightly packed
   mixed greens

1. Season the steaks with salt, then set aside.

2. Prepare the grill for direct-heat grilling, aiming for a grill temperature of 400°F to 450°F.

3. In a blender, make the dressing by combining the avocado oil, lime juice and zest, cilantro, jalapeño, garlic, ginger, fish sauce, mint, and honey. Pulse just long enough to combine but leave some chunks for texture.

4. Sear the steaks for 3 to 4 minutes on each side, shutting the lid on the grill in between turns. The steak should take 8 to 10 minutes for medium-rare, depending on the thickness of the steak. Once the steak has reached your desired internal temperature, or 125°F for medium-rare, remove it from the heat to rest while you assemble the salad.

5. In a large bowl, lightly toss the cucumbers, red onion, and tomatoes with the dressing, reserving some dressing for serving, then add the mixed greens and toss one more time.

6. Divide the salad between two plates. Slice the steak against the grain into ¼-inch-thick slices and top the salads with the steak. Drizzle the reserved dressing over the steak just before serving.

★ Steak Swap: **Flank steak or flat iron steak can be used to make this recipe if you can't find hanger steak.**

Perfect Partner: **Grilled Lemon-Pepper Broccoli (page 95) is a good side dish to serve alongside this beef salad.**

Variation Tip: **This salad can also be served as a wrap or in rice paper wrappers if you want to make a handheld version of this recipe.**

BLUE CHEESE AND BACON CARPETBAGGER

Serves 2   Prep time: 10 minutes   Cook time: 15 minutes

This old-school steak house preparation is a great recipe that you can make at home with just a few ingredients. Stuffing the steak with blue cheese adds a ton of flavor to the mild steak, and the bacon brings an extra element of smoky and salty goodness. The carpetbagger steak originated in small fishing villages in South Wales but became a luxury item in the 1950s and 1960s in Australia. The original recipe was prepared by cutting a small pocket into the steak and stuffing it with a raw oyster. Over the years, the recipe has evolved to steak stuffed with everything from meat and cheese to fresh herbs and seafood.

2 (8-ounce) filets mignons
4 ounces blue cheese crumbles

2 bacon slices
¼ teaspoon kosher salt

¼ teaspoon freshly ground black pepper

1. Prepare the grill for dual-zone cooking with the coals off to one side. Aim for a grill temperature of 400°F to 450°F

2. Using a paring knife, make a small pocket in the side of each filet by cutting into it about three-quarters of the way through, being careful not to cut all the way through. The hole should be just big enough to fill with the cheese. Stuff each steak with 2 ounces of blue cheese, then wrap a slice of bacon around the steak, covering the incision. Use a toothpick to hold the bacon in place, then season the steaks with the salt and pepper.

3. Sear the steaks for 6 to 8 minutes per side for medium-rare, shutting the lid on the grill in between turns. Then quickly sear the steaks for 30 seconds per side before moving them to indirect heat to cook until they reach your desired internal temperature, or 125°F for medium-rare, 12 to 16 minutes, depending on the thickness of the steak.

4. Remove the steaks from the grill and let them rest for 5 minutes before serving the steaks whole.

★ Steak Swap: You can also prepare this recipe with a top sirloin steak, also known as a baseball steak.

Perfect Partner: This is a great dish to serve with Creamed Spinach (page 88).

Variation Tip: If you don't want to stuff the steak, you can cheat and just top the steak with crumbled blue cheese and bacon to get the same flavors.

SOUTH AFRICAN BRAAI-SPICED STEAK

Serves 2   Prep time: 5 minutes, plus 2 hours or overnight to marinate   Cook time: 35 minutes

You might not think of South Africa as a hotbed for grilling enthusiasts, but it is an incredibly popular practice there—and they love beef. Like the term *barbecue, braai* has multiple meanings; it can refer to the actual grill itself or the act of cooking over an open fire. The unique flavors in this spice rub complement the steak with subtle notes of sweetness and spice, creating a beautiful crust on the steaks. I like to prepare the rub the night before and season the steak overnight to dry brine and impart the flavor deep into the meat. If you can't dry brine overnight, a few hours will be fine.

For the spice rub

2 tablespoons kosher salt

1 tablespoon brown sugar

2 teaspoons smoked paprika

1 teaspoon granulated onion

1 teaspoon granulated garlic

1 teaspoon freshly ground
    black pepper

1 teaspoon ground coriander

½ teaspoon dried thyme

½ teaspoon dried rosemary

1 (1½-pound) T-bone steak

1 tablespoon avocado oil

2 tablespoons unsalted
    butter, melted

1. **To make the spice rub:** In a small airtight container, combine the salt, brown sugar, paprika, granulated onion, granulated garlic, pepper, coriander, thyme, and rosemary. Seal the container and shake to combine the ingredients. Brush the steak with the avocado oil, then season liberally with the spice rub. Place the steak in the refrigerator on a cooling rack, uncovered, for at least a few hours, preferably overnight.

2. Prepare the grill for dual-zone cooking with the coals off to one side. Aim for a grill temperature of 400°F to 450°F.

3. Once the grill is up to temperature, take the steak out of the refrigerator and pat it dry on both sides with a paper towel, then lightly re-season using the dry rub.

4. Sear the steak for 2 to 3 minutes per side over direct heat, leaving the grill open to make sure the sugars in the rub don't burn.

5. Once a crust has developed on both sides, move the steak to the side with indirect heat, placing the larger side of the steak closer to the heat source to help it cook evenly. As the steak is cooking over indirect heat, brush with the melted butter. Continue to cook until the steak has reached your desired internal temperature, or 125°F for medium-rare, 17 to 20 minutes, depending on the thickness of the steak. Make sure to take the temperature on both the strip side and the filet side, as they will cook at different times. Remove the steak from the grill and let it rest for 5 minutes.

6. To serve, carve the strip and the filet off the bone, then slice each steak against the grain into $3/4$-inch-thick slices. Serve on a platter or cutting board with the bone, pouring any remaining butter over the steak.

★ Steak Swap: **You can use any steak you prefer with this recipe, but bone-in rib eye or porterhouse would be your best bet.**

Perfect Partner: **Thick-cut Steak House Onion Rings (page 97) would be great with this big juicy steak.**

PICANHA WITH CHIMICHURRI

Serves 4 to 6 Prep time: 15 minutes, plus 2 hours or overnight to marinate
Cook time: 1 hour 15 minutes

Picanha is the cut of choice at Brazilian steak houses and has gained popularity in the United States in recent years. This cut is also known as a sirloin cap or coulotte and comes from the top rump of the cow. Picanha can be seared whole, as in this recipe, but it can also be cut into thick steaks and either grilled or skewered and slow cooked on a rotisserie. Picanha has a large fat cap on top that melts as the meat cooks, basting the meat and keeping it moist throughout the cooking process. Chimichurri is a bright, vibrant sauce commonly served with steak. The sauce requires no cooking and is made with fresh herbs, spices, and oil and served at room temperature.

For the chimichurri

½ cup avocado oil

¼ cup chopped fresh cilantro

¼ cup chopped fresh flat-
  leaf parsley

2 tablespoons white vinegar

5 garlic cloves, peeled

1 jalapeño pepper, seeded

1 teaspoon dried oregano

1 teaspoon kosher salt

½ teaspoon red pepper flakes

---

1 (2- to 3-pound) picanha

1 tablespoon kosher salt

1. **To make the chimichurri:** In a blender, combine the avocado oil, cilantro, parsley, vinegar, garlic, jalapeño, oregano, salt, and red pepper flakes. Pulse just long enough to combine but leave some chunks for texture.

2. To prep the picanha, remove any silver skin from the bottom and then use a sharp knife to score the fat cap in a checkered pattern, making each cut about 1 inch apart. The cuts should be just deep enough to cut through the fat cap and barely cut into the meat.

3. Place the picanha in a large resealable plastic bag and add ¼ cup of the chimichurri sauce. Marinate in the refrigerator for 2 hours or as long as overnight.

4. Prepare the grill for dual-zone cooking with the coals off to one side. Aim for a grill temperature of 350°F to 400°F.

5. Once the grill has come up to temperature, remove the picanha from the bag and pat it dry with paper towels. Season with the salt on all sides.

6. Place the picanha fat-side down over direct heat. Sear for 4 to 5 minutes before flipping over and searing for another 5 minutes. After you have developed a crust on all sides, move the picanha to the indirect side and continue to cook with the lid on until the steak reaches your desired internal temperature, or 125°F for medium-rare, 45 to 55 minutes. Remove the steak from the grill and let it rest for 10 minutes.

7. To serve, slice the steak against the grain into ¼-inch-thick slices. Serve with the chimichurri sauce on the side.

★ Steak Swap: If you can't find picanha, you can substitute it with tri-tip or a sirloin roast.

Perfect Partner: My Jalapeño-Cheddar Mashed Potatoes (page 91) work well with this steak.

Variation Tip: This recipe can also be prepared using the sous vide method (page 24) and then seared on the grill if you have the setup. This method will ensure the meat is perfectly cooked and extra tender.

BAVETTE WITH BURGUNDY SAUCE

Serves 2   Prep time: 5 minutes   Cook time: 30 minutes

Flank steak, also known as bavette, comes from the abdomen of the cow and is one of the most underrated cuts on the market. These tender and incredibly juicy steaks are quite versatile. The burgundy sauce that is paired with this steak complements the bold taste of the meat with mushrooms, garlic, and shallots simmered in butter and red wine, for a restaurant-quality meal in the comfort of your own home.

2 (8-ounce) flank steaks
1 tablespoon avocado oil
¼ teaspoon kosher salt
¼ teaspoon freshly ground
    black pepper

For the sauce
¼ cup finely chopped shallots
4 garlic cloves, minced
3 tablespoons unsalted butter
2 cups sliced mushrooms
3 tablespoons all-purpose flour

1 cup red wine
1 cup beef stock
1 tablespoon Italian seasoning
½ teaspoon salt
½ teaspoon freshly ground
    black pepper

1. Prepare the grill for direct-heat grilling, aiming for a grill temperature of 450°F to 500°F.

2. Brush the steaks with the avocado oil, then season with salt and pepper. Set aside.

3. **To make the sauce:** In a skillet over medium heat, sauté the shallots and garlic in the butter for 2 to 3 minutes, until translucent. Add the mushrooms and cook for an additional 2 minutes, until the mushrooms are soft. Whisk in the flour and cook for about 1 minute.

4. Deglaze the pan with the red wine and beef stock, scraping the bottom of the skillet to release any stuck bits. Simmer the sauce for about 10 minutes, until it has reduced by half and coats the back of a spoon.

5. Add the Italian seasoning, salt, and pepper. Stir, cover, and set aside.

6. Once the grill is hot, sear the steaks for 4 to 5 minutes per side for medium-rare, shutting the lid on the grill in between turns. The steaks should take 8 to 11 minutes to reach medium-rare depending on the thickness of the steak. Once the steaks have reached your desired internal temperature, about 125°F for medium-rare, remove them from the grill and let them rest for 5 minutes.

7. To serve, slice each steak against the grain into 1½-inch-thick slices. Top with the burgundy sauce just before serving.

★ Steak Swap: **This sauce is a perfect pairing with filet or strip steak if you can't find flank steak.**

Perfect Partner: **Burgundy sauce is often served with frites (fries) so you can dip the potatoes in the sauce.**

GRILLED STRIP STEAK
WITH CHARRED TOMATOES

Serves 2   Prep time: 5 minutes   Cook time: 25 minutes

This easy strip steak preparation uses simple seasoning and fresh herbs. The charred tomatoes offer a bright flavor and act as both a side dish and a sauce. Grilling strip steaks over high heat while brushing on butter gives the steak another layer of richness. If you are looking for a great first grilling recipe, this is the perfect place to start.

2 (12-ounce) strip steaks

1 tablespoon avocado oil

1 teaspoon salt, plus more for seasoning

1 teaspoon freshly ground black pepper, plus more for seasoning

2 large beefsteak tomatoes, cut into 8 wedges

4 tablespoons (½ stick) unsalted butter, melted

2 garlic cloves, minced

3 rosemary sprigs, tied together with butcher's twine

1 thyme sprig

1. Prepare the grill for direct-heat grilling, aiming for a grill temperature of 450°F to 500°F.

2. Brush the steaks with the avocado oil, then season with salt and pepper. Set aside.

3. Season the tomatoes with salt and pepper.

4. Combine the melted butter with the minced garlic; using butcher's twine, tie up the rosemary and thyme to make a brush for basting the steaks.

5. Sear the steaks for 3 to 4 minutes per side for medium-rare, shutting the lid on the grill in between turns. Once the steaks have been flipped and are three-quarters cooked, around 100°F for medium-rare, place the tomato slices on the grill and cook for about 2 minutes per side, just long enough to get some chargrilled flavor but not so long that they turn mushy.

6. Once the steaks have reached your desired internal temperature, or 125°F for medium-rare, remove them from the grill. Using the herb brush, baste the steaks with the garlic butter, then let them rest for 5 minutes before serving with the charred tomatoes on the side.

★ Steak Swap: This recipe works great with rib eye or T-bone steaks as well.

Perfect Partner: This is the perfect meal to serve with Grilled Caesar Salad (page 94).

Variation Tip: You can use sirloin or bavette steaks instead of strip steaks with this recipe.

Hoisin-Glazed Sirloin Skewers

3

STEAK UNLEASHED

This chapter is all about taking steak and elevating it. Steak can be presented in countless different ways by adding simple things like herbs and seasoning or pairing it with seafood and sauces that propel it to new heights. These recipes pay tribute to that juicy hunk of beef while bringing in some other flavors to round things out and push the dishes in different directions. Here you will find some of my favorite steak preparations, which I have served both at home and at some of the restaurants I have worked at throughout my career.

Steak Chesapeake 60

Blackened Rib Eye
with Cajun Cream Sauce 62

Steak Caprese 63

Bourbon-Butter Tomahawk Rib Eye 64

Pastrami-Crusted Beef Tenderloin 66

Flat Iron Steak with Tarragon Sauce 68

Denver Steak with Horseradish Sauce 69

Hoisin-Glazed Sirloin Skewers 70

Philly Steak Rib Eye 72

French Onion Steak 73

Jerk-Marinated Tri-Tip 74

Pineapple and Soy Sauce–Marinated
Round Steaks 76

Jalapeño-Popper Pinwheels 78

Steak Benedict 80

Country Fried Steak with Black
Pepper Gravy 82

Steak and Shrimp Scampi 84

STEAK CHESAPEAKE

Serves 4   Prep time: 10 minutes   Cook time: 20 minutes

Steak Chesapeake is the ultimate grilled surf and turf dinner. If you are looking to impress your guests or treat yourself to a truly decadent meal, this is the recipe you need to make—grilled sirloin steak topped with a creamy, rich Chesapeake cream sauce with sautéed mushrooms and tender crabmeat.

4 (6-ounce) sirloin steaks
1 tablespoon avocado oil
½ teaspoon kosher salt
½ teaspoon freshly ground
    black pepper

For the sauce

3 tablespoons unsalted butter
1 cup sliced button mushrooms
2 tablespoons dry sherry or
    sweet vermouth

½ teaspoon Old Bay seasoning
¾ cup heavy (whipping) cream
8 ounces jumbo lump, backfin, or
    claw crabmeat
1 tablespoon chopped
    fresh chives

1. Prepare the grill for dual-zone cooking with the coals off to one side. Aim for a grill temperature of 400°F to 450°F.

2. Brush the steaks with the avocado oil, then season with the salt and pepper on all sides.

3. Sear the steaks for 4 to 5 minutes on each side, shutting the lid on the grill in between turns. Once the steaks have been seared on both sides, move them to the indirect-heat zone to slowly finish cooking while you prepare the Chesapeake sauce.

4. **To make the sauce:** Place a skillet on the hot zone of the grill, melt the butter in it, then sauté the mushrooms for 3 to 4 minutes, until tender.

5. Deglaze the pan with the sherry, stirring to scrape up the browned bits from the bottom.

6. Add the Old Bay seasoning. Pour in the heavy cream and cook for 3 to 4 minutes, until the sauce is reduced by half and coats the back of a spoon. Remove from the direct heat and gently fold in the crabmeat and chives. The carryover heat of the sauce will warm the crabmeat.

7. The steaks should take a total of 8 to 11 minutes to reach medium-rare, depending on the thickness of the steaks. Once they have reached your desired internal temperature, or 125°F for medium-rare, remove them from the grill and let them rest for 5 minutes.

8. Top the steaks with the Chesapeake sauce and serve.

★ Steak Swap: You can prepare this recipe with any cut that you cook to temperature. Filet mignon or strip steak would be my personal choice for a great substitution.

Perfect Partner: Serve with grilled veggies or Garlic-Herb Hasselback Potatoes (page 89).

Variation Tip: Sometimes crabmeat can be hard to find or expensive. You can substitute shrimp to make this dish a little more affordable.

BLACKENED RIB EYE WITH CAJUN CREAM SAUCE

Serves 2   Prep time: 10 minutes   Cook time: 20 minutes

This dish is a fantastic way to showcase all the flavors of the Big Easy. Coating the rib eye in Cajun seasoning gives the steak a salty and spicy crust that chars up nicely on the grill. Topped with a rich cream sauce, this steak gives you the flavor of the bayou on a grill.

1 (16-ounce) boneless or 1 (1½-pound) bone-in rib eye
½ tablespoon Cajun seasoning

For the sauce
2 tablespoons unsalted butter

½ cup finely diced onions
½ cup finely diced bell pepper
2 garlic cloves, minced
¾ cup heavy (whipping) cream

1 tablespoon chopped fresh parsley
2 teaspoons Tabasco or other hot sauce
½ teaspoon Cajun seasoning

1. Prepare the grill for direct-heat grilling, aiming for a grill temperature of 450°F to 500°F.

2. While the grill is heating, season the steak with the Cajun seasoning on both sides.

3. **To make the sauce:** In a medium sauté pan or skillet, melt the butter over medium heat. Add the onions, peppers, and garlic and cook for 2 minutes, until softened.

4. Add the heavy cream to the pan and cook for about 2 minutes, or until the sauce has thickened and coats the back of a spoon. Stir in the parsley, Tabasco, and Cajun seasoning. Remove from the heat and set aside.

5. Sear the steak for 4 to 5 minutes per side, or until a dark crust forms. Rotate the steak away from any flare-ups as needed, shutting the lid on the grill in between turns. For medium-rare, cook for a total of 8 to 11 minutes, depending on the thickness of the steak. Once the steak has reached your desired internal temperature, or 125°F for medium-rare, remove it from the grill and let it rest for 5 minutes.

6. Transfer the steak to a serving platter, top with the sauce, and serve.

★ Steak Swap: **Flat iron, hangar, and strip steak are optimal substitutes for the rib eye in this recipe.**

Perfect Partner: **I love to serve this steak with Rosemary-Truffle Fries (page 93) or mini Garlic-Herb Hasselback Potatoes (page 89).**

Variation Tip: **If sharing, you can slice the rib eye into strips after it has rested and pour the sauce over each portion.**

STEAK CAPRESE

Serves 4   Prep time: 10 minutes   Cook time: 30 minutes

This delicious recipe takes perfectly grilled and sliced flank steak and tops it with ripe tomatoes and fresh mozzarella cheese like its namesake salad. A final drizzle of balsamic vinegar gives the dish a rich acidic balance. I love serving this on a beautiful summer day with a glass of wine. If you love Italian cuisine, then you'll love this recipe.

2 beefsteak tomatoes

8 ounces fresh mozzarella cheese

8 to 10 fresh basil leaves

1 (16-ounce) flank steak

3 tablespoons olive oil

1 teaspoon Italian seasoning

1 teaspoon kosher salt

½ teaspoon freshly ground black pepper

1 tablespoon balsamic glaze

1. Prepare the grill for dual-zone cooking with the coals off to one side. Aim for a grill temperature of 350°F to 400°F.

2. Slice the tomatoes and mozzarella cheese into ¼-inch-thick slices and set aside. Roll the basil leaves up, then slice thinly into ribbons.

3. Brush the flank steak with the olive oil, then season with the Italian seasoning, salt, and pepper on both sides.

4. Sear the flank steak for 2 to 3 minutes per side over direct heat, shutting the lid on the grill in between turns.

5. Once the steak is seared to rare, move it to the indirect side and layer on the tomatoes and mozzarella cheese. Close the lid on the grill and cook for an additional 2 to 3 minutes to melt the cheese and allow the steak to reach medium-rare with an internal temperature of 125°F. Remove the steak from the grill and let it rest for 5 minutes.

6. To serve, slice the flank steak into 4 sections, drizzle with the balsamic glaze, and top with the fresh basil.

★ Steak Swap: If you can't find flank steak, you can also use a flat iron steak.

Perfect Partner: Prosciutto-Wrapped Brussels Sprouts (page 90) are a fantastic side dish with this recipe.

Variation Tip: If you don't like warm tomatoes, you can serve the tomato and mozzarella chilled on the side.

BOURBON-BUTTER TOMAHAWK RIB EYE

Serves 4   Prep time: 10 minutes   Cook time: 1 hour

The tomahawk rib eye is hands down one of the most impressive steaks, and it needs to be treated with care. First off, you are paying a lot of money for that massive bone, which really doesn't serve any purpose other than presentation, so you'll want to be sure it doesn't come out burnt. To ensure that this steak is cooked perfectly, I recommend reverse searing. Slowly bring the steak up to temperature before searing it quickly over hot coals. To finish off this beautiful dinosaur steak, I brush it with a simple bourbon butter that brings a slightly sweet, oaky taste to the steak.

1 (3-pound) tomahawk rib eye
2 tablespoons avocado oil
1 teaspoon kosher salt
1 teaspoon freshly ground
   black pepper

1 teaspoon paprika
½ teaspoon granulated garlic
½ teaspoon granulated onion

For the bourbon butter

4 tablespoons (½ stick) unsalted
   butter, at room temperature
1 ounce bourbon
1 tablespoon brown sugar
1 teaspoon hot sauce

1. Preheat the oven to 250°F and prepare the grill for direct-heat grilling, aiming for a grill temperature of 450°F to 500°F.

2. Wrap the bone of the tomahawk rib eye with aluminum foil to protect it from burning. In a small bowl, combine the avocado oil, salt, pepper, paprika, granulated garlic, and granulated onion. Stir to form a wet paste, then spread it all over the steak.

3. Place a cooking rack on a baking sheet and set the steak on the rack. Cook in the oven for 30 to 40 minutes, or until it reaches an internal temperature of 125°F for medium-rare. Remove from the oven and let it rest for 5 minutes.

4. **To make the bourbon butter:** While the steak is in the oven, in a small saucepan over medium-low heat, combine the butter, bourbon, brown sugar, and hot sauce and cook until the butter has melted and the sugar is dissolved, about 2 minutes.

5. Once the steak has rested for 5 minutes and the grill is heated to searing temperature, sear the steak on the grill for 1 to 2 minutes with the lid open, then flip to sear the other side for another 1 to 2 minutes.

6. After the first flip, brush the bourbon butter on the steak. Remove the steak from the grill and baste it on the other side with more butter.

7. To serve, carve the steak by removing it from the bone, then slice it against the grain into ¼-inch-thick slices. Brush with any remaining bourbon butter just before serving.

★ Steak Swap: You can substitute a cowboy cut or any bone-in rib eye.

Perfect Partner: Jalapeño-Cheddar Mashed Potatoes (page 91) is the perfect side dish for this tomahawk rib eye.

Variation Tip: If you have a smoker, you can smoke the rib eye instead of baking it in the oven before searing.

PASTRAMI-CRUSTED BEEF TENDERLOIN

Serves 6   Prep time: 5 minutes, plus 6 to 48 hours to marinate   Cook time: 1 hour 15 minutes

This is a fantastic recipe for those who love the flavor of pastrami but want a perfectly grilled steak at the same time. Dry brining imparts flavor deep into the beef and creates a beautiful crust. If you are not comfortable trimming a whole tenderloin, ask your butcher or the person working the counter at the grocery store to cut you a 3-pound center-cut tenderloin. Bonus points if they tie it for you, which will help the steak hold its shape and cook more evenly, but that is optional.

1 (3-pound) center-cut beef tenderloin

2 tablespoons Dijon mustard

2 tablespoons freshly ground black pepper

1 tablespoon coarsely ground coriander

1 tablespoon kosher salt

1. Brush the entire tenderloin with the Dijon mustard. In a small bowl, combine the pepper, coriander, and salt and season the beef liberally on all sides with the mixture.

2. Set the tenderloin on a cooling rack on top of a sheet pan to catch any moisture and place the tenderloin, uncovered, in the refrigerator to dry brine for up to 48 hours, or as little as 6 hours for a milder flavor.

3. Prepare the grill for dual-zone cooking with the coals off to one side. Aim for a grill temperature of 350°F to 400°F.

4. Place the tenderloin on the indirect side of the grill, cover, and cook for about 1 hour, or until it reaches an internal temperature of 120°F. You may need to add charcoal to maintain the temperature.

5. Once the tenderloin has reached 120°F, open the lid of the grill and rake the coals to get them extra hot for searing, then move the tenderloin to the direct-heat side and sear for about 3 minutes on each side, leaving the lid open, until the outside of the tenderloin is seared on all sides with a dark crust and the internal temperature reaches 125°F for medium-rare. Remove the steak from the grill and let it rest for 5 to 10 minutes.

6. Slice the steak against the grain into $\frac{1}{2}$-inch-thick medallions and serve.

★ Steak swap: **You can use this same method to prepare individual filet mignon steaks.**

Perfect Partner: **Although it might seem odd, I love to serve this steak with sauerkraut or coleslaw alongside spicy mustard.**

Variation Tip: **If you don't have time to dry brine overnight, that's okay, but try to refrigerate it for at least 4 to 6 hours so the seasoning has time to adhere to the beef.**

FLAT IRON STEAK WITH TARRAGON SAUCE

Serves 2   Prep time: 10 minutes   Cook time: 25 minutes

Tarragon is a fresh herb that you don't see often in steak recipes, but I love its unique anise flavor as a counterpoint to the richness of beef. Using the tarragon in a cream sauce allows you to control the intensity of the flavor so you can make it as strong or as mild as you like. You can also use this sauce with chicken or fish for any guests that might not eat beef.

2 (8-ounce) flat iron steaks
1 teaspoon kosher salt
1 teaspoon freshly ground
   black pepper

For the sauce

2 tablespoons unsalted butter
2 garlic cloves, minced
1 shallot, minced
2 ounces dry vermouth

½ cup heavy (whipping) cream
2 tablespoons thinly
   sliced fresh tarragon
⅛ teaspoon kosher salt
½ teaspoon freshly ground
   black pepper

1. Prepare the grill for direct-heat grilling, aiming for a grill temperature of 450°F to 500°F.

2. Season the steaks on both sides with the salt and pepper and set aside at room temperature while preparing the sauce.

3. **To make the sauce:** In a small saucepan, melt the butter over medium heat. Add the garlic and shallots. Cook for about 3 minutes, until softened, then deglaze the pan with the vermouth, scraping the bottom of the pan to release any stuck bits.

4. Add the heavy cream and tarragon to the pan and cook for 3 to 4 minutes, until the sauce thickens enough to coat the back of a spoon. Season with the salt and pepper, then remove from the heat.

5. Sear the steaks for 4 to 5 minutes per side, shutting the lid on the grill in between turns. For medium-rare, cook for a total of 8 to 11 minutes, depending on the thickness of the steaks. Once the steaks have reached your desired internal temperature, or 125°F for medium-rare, remove them from the grill and let them rest for 5 minutes.

6. Top the steaks with the tarragon sauce and serve.

★ Steak Swap: **Use flank steak or Denver steak in place of flat iron for this recipe.**

Perfect Partner: **This dish is fantastic with Mushroom Risotto (page 92).**

Variation Tip: **If using dry tarragon, use 2 teaspoons.**

DENVER STEAK
WITH HORSERADISH SAUCE

Serves 2   Prep time: 10 minutes   Cook time: 15 minutes

Even though this is a simple recipe, I promise it doesn't hold back in the flavor department. Horseradish cream is often served with prime rib, but this sauce is outstanding with just about any cut of beef. Denver steaks are a fairly new cut with beautiful marbling, great for searing over a hot fire. Slicing the steak makes for a stunning presentation and lets you double-check the steaks' internal temperature.

For the sauce

½ cup mayonnaise

¼ cup sour cream

¼ cup prepared horseradish

Juice of 1 lemon

1 teaspoon Worcestershire sauce

1 teaspoon freshly ground
   black pepper

2 (8-ounce) Denver steaks

1 tablespoon avocado oil

½ teaspoon kosher salt

½ teaspoon freshly ground
   black pepper

1. **To make the sauce:** In a small bowl, whisk together the mayonnaise, sour cream, horseradish, lemon juice, Worcestershire sauce, and pepper. Once incorporated, refrigerate for 30 minutes while you prepare the grill and cook the steaks.

2. Prepare the grill for direct-heat grilling, aiming for a grill temperature of 450°F to 500°F.

3. Brush the steaks with the avocado oil, then season with the salt and pepper.

4. Sear the steaks for 4 to 5 minutes per side, shutting the lid on the grill in between turns. For medium-rare, cook for 8 to 11 minutes, depending on the thickness of the steak. Once the steaks have reached your desired internal temperature, or 125°F for medium-rare, remove them from the grill and let them rest for 5 minutes.

5. To serve, slice the steaks against the grain into ¼-inch-thick slices. Serve the horseradish sauce on the side.

★ Steak Swap: **This recipe is great for any steak you cook to temperature. The closest substitute for a Denver steak would be a flat iron or flank steak.**

Perfect Partner: **I love to serve this recipe with Garlic-Herb Hasselback Potatoes (page 89).**

Variation Tip: **Instead of a cold horseradish sauce, you can prepare a warm sauce using heavy cream and butter.**

HOISIN-GLAZED SIRLOIN SKEWERS

Serves 4   Prep time: 10 minutes, plus 2 hours or overnight to marinate   Cook time: 10 minutes

These skewers make for a mouthwatering appetizer. They can also be served over rice as a main course. The combination of the fresh ginger and garlic, along with the chopped cilantro, gives the steak a punch of freshness. The sweet and salty components of the marinade come from the soy sauce and the hoisin. Hoisin sauce is a thick, sweet sauce that is associated with Peking duck but can be used in a variety of recipes.

For the marinade

Juice and zest of 2 limes

¼ cup chopped fresh cilantro

2 tablespoons soy sauce

2 tablespoons hoisin sauce

2 tablespoons rice wine vinegar or white vinegar

1 tablespoon sriracha

1 tablespoon sesame oil

1 tablespoon grated fresh ginger

4 garlic cloves, minced

½ teaspoon Chinese five-spice powder

1 pound sirloin tips, cut into 2-inch cubes

1. **To make the marinade:** In a large bowl, whisk together the lime juice and zest, cilantro, soy sauce, hoisin sauce, vinegar, sriracha, sesame oil, ginger, garlic, and five-spice powder.

2. Add the cubed sirloin to the bowl and toss to make sure the beef is completely coated with the marinade. Cover and refrigerate for at least 2 hours, or as long as overnight.

3. While the meat is marinating, soak 6-inch bamboo skewers in water so they don't burn while grilling.

4. After the meat has marinated, place 3 pieces of meat on each skewer. Reserve the marinade for basting.

5. Prepare the grill for direct-heat grilling, aiming for a grill temperature of 350°F to 400°F.

6. Place the skewers on the outer edges of the heat so that the handles of the skewers don't burn. Sear for 3 to 4 minutes per side, shutting the lid on the grill in between turns.

7. Once the skewers have been seared on all sides, brush the meat with the remaining marinade. Cook for an additional 2 minutes and then remove the skewers from the grill. The skewers will be cooked somewhere between medium and medium-well. Because the steak pieces are small, it will be hard to cook to temperature, but the internal temperature should register between 130°F and 140°F.

8. Let the sirloin rest for 2 to 3 minutes before serving.

★ Steak Swap: **For even more tender meat, use strip steaks cut into 2-inch cubes.**

Perfect Partner: **Serve these sirloin skewers over white rice or riced cauliflower.**

Variation Tip: **You can add onion or pepper slices in between each piece of beef on the skewers for an extra crunch and beautiful color.**

PHILLY STEAK RIB EYE

Serves 4   Prep time: 10 minutes   Cook time: 30 minutes

Having visited Philadelphia many times to enjoy its iconic sandwich, I have strong feelings about cheesesteaks. If you are like me and think Philly cheesesteaks are better with provolone than Cheez Whiz, then you will love this recipe. Most cheesesteaks are made with shaved rib eye because it has great texture and marbling, so why not just grill a rib eye and top it with peppers, onions, and provolone? It's a great weeknight meal because the onions and peppers serve as the side, making this a one-dish dinner.

3 tablespoons unsalted butter

1 large white onion, sliced

1 red bell pepper, seeded and sliced

1 green bell pepper, seeded and sliced

2 (12-ounce) boneless rib eye steaks

1 teaspoon kosher salt

1 teaspoon freshly ground black pepper

6 slices provolone cheese

1. Prepare the grill for direct-heat grilling, aiming for a grill temperature of 450°F to 500°F.

2. In a cast-iron skillet on the grill, melt the butter, then add the onions and peppers. Cook for 5 to 8 minutes, or until the onions and peppers are tender but not mushy.

3. Once the onions and peppers are about halfway done, season the steaks with the salt and pepper.

4. Sear the steaks for 3 to 4 minutes per side, shutting the lid on the grill in between turns.

5. After flipping the steaks, when they are about three-quarters done, top each steak with half the onions, half the peppers, and 3 slices of provolone cheese. Close the lid of the grill and cook for about 2 minutes, or just until the cheese is melted and the steaks' internal temperature is 125°F for medium-rare. Serve immediately.

★ Steak Swap: You can prepare this recipe using sirloin or strip steaks if you are looking for a more affordable cut.

Perfect Partner: I would serve this dish with some crispy Rosemary-Truffle Fries (page 93).

Variation Tip: This dish can also be prepared all in the cast-iron skillet by searing the steaks in one side of the pan while the peppers and onions cook on the other side. Top with provolone at the end.

FRENCH ONION STEAK

Serves 2   Prep time: 15 minutes   Cook time: 35 minutes

If you love French onion soup for all its cheesy goodness and caramelized onions, then imagine layering those amazing ingredients over a juicy steak. The tender flank steak pairs perfectly with the onions and broth, which add so much flavor to the steak. This recipe comes straight from my chef's playbook; it was always a customer favorite at my restaurant, and I know you'll love it, too.

For the sauce

3 tablespoons unsalted butter

1 yellow onion, thinly sliced

½ teaspoon chopped
   fresh thyme

2 teaspoons tomato paste

¼ cup beef broth or stock

¼ cup red wine

1 tablespoon
   Worcestershire sauce

2 (8-ounce) flank steaks

½ teaspoon kosher salt

½ teaspoon freshly ground
   black pepper

½ cup shredded Gruyère cheese

1. **To make the sauce:** In a medium skillet over medium-low heat, melt the butter. Add the onions and thyme and cook, stirring occasionally, for around 20 minutes, or until the onions are completely caramelized. Then add the tomato paste and cook for 1 minute before pouring in the beef broth, red wine, and Worcestershire sauce.

2. Cook the sauce down for 10 to 15 minutes, or until most of the liquid is gone. Remove from the heat and set aside while you prepare the steaks.

3. Prepare the grill for direct-heat grilling, aiming for a grill temperature of around 450°F.

4. Season the steaks with the salt and pepper on both sides.

5. Sear for about 4 minutes per side for medium-rare, shutting the lid on the grill in between turns.

6. Once the steaks have reached 120°F, use a spatula to create a well for each steak in the skillet with the onions. Place the steaks in the skillet and top each steak with half of the caramelized onions and half of the Gruyère cheese. Place the skillet on the grill, close the lid, and cook for about 5 minutes, until the cheese is melted. For extra-crispy golden cheese, broil the steaks in the oven for 1 to 2 minutes. Keep an eye on the steaks because they can burn quickly.

7. Let the steaks rest for 5 minutes before serving.

★ Steak Swap: **You can substitute strip steak, flat iron, or hanger steak for the flank steak in this recipe.**

Perfect Partner: **Grilled Caesar Salad (page 94) is my go-to side dish for this recipe.**

Variation Tip: **You can use provolone, Swiss, or even Brie cheese in place of the Gruyère.**

JERK-MARINATED TRI-TIP

Serves 4 to 6   Prep time: 10 minutes, plus 2 hours or overnight to marinate
Cook time: 1 hour 15 minutes

Tri-tip is a large roast that has a boomerang shape and is best served between medium or medium-rare. Because of its shape, its grain runs in two directions. When slicing, be sure to cut the roast in half at the juncture, then slice each piece against its grain. This recipe uses an herbaceous jerk rub with Caribbean spices. The tri-tip is slow roasted over indirect heat until almost finished and then seared just before serving. It's basically the reverse-sear method but all on the grill.

For the jerk seasoning

2 teaspoons kosher salt

1 teaspoon freshly ground black pepper

1 teaspoon smoked paprika

½ teaspoon dried thyme

½ teaspoon dried rosemary

½ teaspoon ground allspice

½ teaspoon ground cinnamon

½ teaspoon ground cloves

½ teaspoon ground ginger

¼ teaspoon ground nutmeg

¼ cup avocado oil

¼ cup roughly chopped scallions, both white and green parts

2 tablespoons soy sauce

6 garlic cloves, peeled

1 (3-pound) tri-tip roast

1. **To make the jerk seasoning:** In a small bowl, combine the salt, pepper, paprika, thyme, rosemary, allspice, cinnamon, cloves, ginger, and nutmeg.

2. In a blender, combine the avocado oil, scallions, soy sauce, and garlic. Puree until smooth, then add the jerk seasoning and pulse to combine into a paste.

3. Smear the paste all over the tri-tip. Refrigerate the tri-tip, uncovered, for about 2 hours, or as long as overnight.

4. Prepare the grill for dual-zone cooking with the coals off to one side. Aim for a grill temperature of around 400°F.

5. Place the tri-tip over indirect heat and cook with the lid closed for about 1 hour, or until the roast reaches an internal temperature of 120°F.

6. Move the tri-tip to the direct heat and sear for about 30 seconds to 1 minute on each side. For optimal texture, serve the tri-tip between medium-rare and medium, or 125°F to 135°F. Once the roast has reached your desired internal temperature, remove it from the grill and let it rest for 10 minutes.

7. Cut the tri-tip in half at the point of the boomerang, then slice the roast against the grain into ¼-inch-thick slices and serve.

★ Steak Swap: **Eye of round roast would be a perfect substitute in this recipe. Slice it thinly before serving.**

Perfect Partner: **Serve with grilled pineapple and grilled veggies of your choice.**

Variation Tip: **Since you'll be cooking this roast for over an hour, add some wood chips to give the tri-tip a smoked flavor.**

PINEAPPLE AND SOY SAUCE- MARINATED ROUND STEAKS

Serves 4   Prep time: 10 minutes, plus 2 hours to marinate   Cook time: 20 minutes

Round steaks can be a great value, but they can also be a very tough cut. To tenderize these lean steaks, I use a couple of secret weapons—pineapple juice and a Jaccard—to help get the marinade deep into the steaks. In just two hours, the pineapple juice can make these tough steaks tender and juicy. With the cilantro, soy sauce, and other flavorful ingredients, this marinade really gives the steak a complete flavor and textural makeover. If you don't have a Jaccard, you can use a fork to poke holes in the steaks.

For the marinade

1 cup pineapple juice

¼ cup soy sauce

¼ cup thinly sliced scallions, both white and green parts

Juice and zest of 2 limes

2 tablespoons chopped fresh cilantro

1 jalapeño pepper, seeded and chopped

1 teaspoon kosher salt

4 (8-ounce) round steaks

1 teaspoon kosher salt

1 teaspoon freshly ground black pepper

1. **To make the marinade:** In a large mixing bowl, combine the pineapple juice, soy sauce, scallions, lime juice and zest, cilantro, jalapeño, and salt.

2. Season the steaks on both sides with the salt and pepper, then use a Jaccard or a fork to perforate the steaks to allow the marinade to penetrate the meat. Submerge the steaks in the marinade, cover, and place in the refrigerator for about 2 hours to tenderize.

3. Prepare the grill for direct-heat grilling, aiming for a grill temperature of around 450°F.

4. Remove the steaks from the marinade, reserving the excess marinade, then pat the steaks dry with paper towels.

5. Pour the remaining marinade into a small saucepan and simmer over medium heat for 5 to 7 minutes, until the sauce reduces by half and becomes thick and sticky. Set aside to cool.

6. Sear the steaks for 4 to 5 minutes per side, shutting the lid on the grill in between turns. After the first turn, brush on some of the reduced marinade on both sides of the steaks so that it can caramelize. Cook for 8 to 11 minutes for medium-rare, depending on the thickness of the steaks. Once the steaks have reached your desired internal temperature, or 125°F for medium-rare, remove them from the grill and let them rest for 5 minutes.

7. Thinly slice the steaks against the grain. Brush with any remaining marinade before serving to keep the steaks from drying out.

★ Steak Swap: **Use skirt or flank steak for a more tender steak.**

Perfect Partner: **This recipe is great over a bed of white rice or with your favorite grilled veggies.**

Variation Tip: **To create a pineapple barbecue sauce to brush the steaks with, add ½ cup of your favorite barbecue sauce to the marinade while you're reducing it in the saucepan.**

JALAPEÑO-POPPER PINWHEELS

Serves 2   Prep time: 15 minutes   Cook time: 30 minutes

This is a fun steak that makes for a great presentation. The skirt steak is smeared with a jalapeño–cream cheese filling and then rolled up and grilled. Make sure to use bamboo skewers or butcher's twine to hold the pinwheels together. If you like super-hot peppers, you can add a tablespoon of chipotle pepper in adobo sauce to the cream cheese mixture. If you prefer mild dishes, you can skip the jalapeño peppers altogether. Either way, the cream cheese mixture keeps the steaks extra moist and juicy.

8 ounces cream cheese, at room temperature

½ cup shredded cheddar cheese

2 jalapeño peppers, seeded and diced

1 (1-pound) skirt steak

½ teaspoon kosher salt

½ teaspoon freshly ground black pepper

1. In a small bowl, mix together the cream cheese, cheddar cheese, and jalapeño until smooth. Set aside.

2. Lay out the skirt steak and trim the steak so that it is a long, even rectangle. Save the trimmings for a stir-fry. Season the steak on both sides with the salt and pepper, then spread the cream cheese mixture out as one even layer, covering the entire skirt steak except for a 1-inch strip on one short end.

3. Roll the skirt steak up, starting on the side with the cream cheese at the edge so that the strip that doesn't have cream cheese is the last part to roll up. Place two bamboo skewers into the pinwheel, one on each end, to hold the steak in place or tie it up with butcher's twine.

4. Slice the pinwheel down the middle in between the skewers so you have two even pinwheels. Chill the steaks in the refrigerator while the grill preheats.

5. Prepare the grill for dual-zone cooking with the coals off to one side. Aim for a grill temperature of around 400°F.

6. Sear the pinwheels for about 4 minutes per side for medium, shutting the lid on the grill in between turns.

7. Once seared on both sides, move the pinwheels to the side with indirect heat and cook for another 15 minutes, or until they reach an internal temperature of 135°F for medium. Remove the pinwheels to a platter, cover them with a sheet of aluminum foil, and let them rest for 10 minutes.

8. Remove the skewers or string from the pinwheels and serve.

★ Steak Swap: **You can use flank steak instead of skirt steak. Just butterfly the flank steak and flatten it out with a meat mallet before preparing.**

Perfect Partner: **Serve with Jalapeño-Cheddar Mashed Potatoes (page 91).**

Variation Tip: **Instead of rolling the steaks into pinwheels, you can cut a pocket in a flank steak and stuff it with the cream cheese mixture before grilling.**

STEAK BENEDICT

Serves 2   Prep time: 15 minutes   Cook time: 20 minutes

Although we tend to think of dinner as the ideal time for grilling, a weekend brunch is actually a great time to make steak on the grill. This craveable twist on steak and eggs is a classy crowd-pleaser, and the entire recipe can be prepared on the grill by toasting the English muffins and warming the ham gently over indirect heat while the steaks and eggs cook over the direct heat. This is a fun version of a classic brunch staple.

For the faux hollandaise sauce

½ cup heavy (whipping) cream
½ teaspoon ground turmeric
1 teaspoon Tabasco sauce

1 teaspoon freshly squeezed lemon juice
3 tablespoons unsalted butter

2 English muffins
4 ounces sliced ham
2 (6-ounce) hanger steaks
½ teaspoon kosher salt
½ teaspoon freshly ground black pepper
1 tablespoon avocado oil
2 large eggs

1. Prepare the grill for dual-zone cooking with the coals off to one side. Aim for a grill temperature of around 400°F.

2. **To make the faux hollandaise sauce:** In a small saucepan over direct heat, reduce the heavy cream along with the turmeric, Tabasco, lemon juice, and butter for about 5 minutes, until the sauce has thickened and coats the back of a spoon. Once the sauce is ready, move the saucepan to the indirect heat and stir occasionally.

3. Toast the English muffins by splitting them and setting them on the indirect side of the grill along with the sliced ham.

4. Season the steaks with the salt and pepper and sear over direct heat for about 4 minutes per side for medium-rare, shutting the lid on the grill in between turns. Cook until the steaks reach the desired internal temperature, 8 to 11 minutes for medium rare, depending on thickness, or 125°F. Remove the steaks from the grill and let them rest for 5 minutes.

5. While the steaks are grilling, place a small skillet over the direct-heat side of the grill and heat the avocado oil. Once the pan is hot, cook the eggs for about 2 minutes per side and then move the pan to the indirect side to rest.

6. Once the steaks are cooked, assemble the Benedict. Start by placing the English muffins open-faced on a plate, then top with the steaks, ham, eggs, and sauce. Serve immediately.

★ Steak Swap: **You may substitute ½-inch slices of beef tenderloin in place of the sirloin steaks.**

Perfect Partner: **Serve with fresh fruit or home fries.**

Variation Tip: **You can also prepare traditional poached eggs for this recipe if you are looking for a more classic Benedict.**

COUNTRY FRIED STEAK
WITH BLACK PEPPER GRAVY

Serves 4   Prep time: 15 minutes   Cook time: 20 minutes

Country fried steak is the epitome of Southern comfort food with thin cuts of tenderized, panfried beef with a crispy crust that's topped with a creamy sauce loaded with lots of black pepper. It's also one of my favorite recipes to make campfire style in a cast-iron skillet over an open flame. You can obviously make this recipe on the stovetop, but making it on the grill gives an added sense of authenticity and accomplishment.

For the black pepper gravy

2 tablespoons unsalted butter
2 tablespoons all-purpose flour
1 cup milk
½ cup heavy (whipping) cream
2 teaspoons Tabasco or other hot sauce

1 teaspoon freshly ground black pepper

Canola oil, for frying
4 (6-ounce) cube steaks
½ cup buttermilk

2 large eggs
½ cup all-purpose flour
½ teaspoon kosher salt
½ teaspoon freshly ground black pepper

1. Prepare the grill for direct-heat grilling, aiming for a grill temperature of around 375°F.

2. **To make the black pepper gravy:** Place a small skillet on the grill and melt the butter. Whisk in the flour and cook for about 1 minute, then add the milk, cream, Tabasco, and pepper. Cook for about 5 minutes, until the gravy is thickened and coats the back of a spoon.

3. In a large oven-safe skillet, pour just enough oil to cover the entire bottom of the skillet. Place the skillet on the grill to heat up while you prepare the steaks.

4. In a small bowl, whisk together the buttermilk and eggs. In another bowl, combine the flour, salt, and pepper.

5. Dredge each steak first in the buttermilk mixture and then in the seasoned flour so that each piece of beef is well coated.

6. Use a probe thermometer to make sure the oil is around 350°F, then carefully place each breaded steak into the pan away from you to avoid splashing the oil. Cook for about 3 minutes per side, until golden and crispy on both sides. Keep the lid of the grill open for the entire

cooking process. Because the steaks are so thin, country fried steak is served medium-well to well-done, so don't worry about overcooking them. Just focus on developing a golden outer crust.

7. Once the steaks are crispy on both sides, remove them from the pan and place them on a paper towel–lined plate to soak up any excess grease. Serve the steaks with the pepper gravy on top or on the side.

★ Steak Swap: **You can use any thin-cut beef for this recipe. Sirloin would also work.**

Perfect Partner: **Serve with grits or some homemade biscuits.**

Variation Tip: **For an extra-thick coating, double dredge the steaks by repeating the dredging step a second time before frying. You will need to double the amount of buttermilk, eggs, flour, salt, and pepper.**

STEAK AND SHRIMP SCAMPI

Serves 2   Prep time: 15 minutes   Cook time: 15 minutes

This is my version of a very simple surf and turf. Shrimp are much more affordable than lobster, and they're easier to cook. Both the steak and the shrimp are grilled and basted with a fantastic lemon butter to create a mouthwatering masterpiece. Grilling the shrimp over an open fire sears in that slightly sweet, briny flavor that makes shrimp one of my favorite types of seafood. Skewering the shrimp makes them easier to handle on the grill so you don't have to flip them individually.

For the scampi butter

8 tablespoons (1 stick) unsalted butter

2 tablespoons avocado oil

Juice of 1 lemon (about 3 tablespoons)

4 garlic cloves, minced

½ tablespoon chopped fresh parsley

1 teaspoon Italian seasoning

1 teaspoon red pepper flakes (optional)

2 (12-ounce) strip steaks

8 ounces large shrimp, peeled and deveined

2 tablespoons avocado oil

1 teaspoon kosher salt

1 teaspoon freshly ground black pepper

½ teaspoon granulated garlic

1. **To make the scampi butter:** In a small saucepan over medium heat, whisk together the butter, avocado oil, lemon juice, garlic, parsley, Italian seasoning, and red pepper flakes (if using) and cook for about 1 minute, just until melted. Remove from the heat and set aside.

2. Soak two bamboo skewers in water for 30 minutes and then place half of the shrimp on each skewer. If the skewers are not long enough, use extra skewers.

3. Prepare the grill for dual-zone cooking with the coals off to one side. Aim for a grill temperature of around 450°F.

4. Brush the steaks and shrimp with the avocado oil, then season both sides with salt, pepper, and granulated garlic.

5. Sear the steaks over direct heat for 4 minutes per side, shutting the lid on the grill in between turns. After the steaks are seared, move them to the indirect side and begin basting them with the garlic butter. Cook for 8 to 11 minutes for medium-rare, depending on the thickness of the steaks, or until the internal temperature reaches 125°F.

6. As soon as the steaks are moved to indirect heat, place the shrimp over direct heat and grill for 2 to 3 minutes per side with the lid open. Brush the shrimp after each turn with the garlic butter. The steak and shrimp should be done at about the same time and can be removed to rest for 5 minutes.

7. Brush any remaining garlic butter on the steaks and shrimp and serve.

★ Steak Swap: **You can use flat iron or hanger steak in place of the strip steak.**

Perfect Partner: **This recipe is amazing with Grilled Lemon-Pepper Broccoli (page 95).**

Variation Tip: **If you really want to splurge, you can split a lobster tail in half and grill it for 5 minutes per side in the shell, brushing it with the garlic butter.**

Creamed Spinach

4

STEAK HOUSE SIDES

As much as I love steak, I can get just as excited about the side dishes. A good side dish should complement the steak and act as a supporting cast member without stealing the show. If you have a rich, fatty steak, you may want to serve it with a light salad or grilled vegetable. Likewise, if you are grilling a leaner cut, you might want to serve something a bit richer like creamed spinach or my personal favorite, mac and cheese. Potatoes are a steak's best friend and perfect for just about any meal, so it's always a good idea to serve spuds with steak.

Creamed Spinach 88

Garlic-Herb Hasselback Potatoes 89

Prosciutto-Wrapped Brussels Sprouts 90

Jalapeño-Cheddar Mashed Potatoes 91

Mushroom Risotto 92

Rosemary-Truffle Fries 93

Grilled Caesar Salad 94

Grilled Lemon-Pepper Broccoli 95

Classic Mac and Cheese 96

Steak House Onion Rings 97

CREAMED SPINACH

Serves 4   Prep time: 10 minutes   Cook time: 15 minutes

Creamy and rich, creamed spinach is a steak house classic side dish that can also double as a sauce to complement a steak. I love to serve creamed spinach alongside steaks that don't have a sauce or are seasoned with only salt and pepper. My personal twist on this classic recipe is to use ricotta cheese instead of a roux or cream cheese. The ricotta gives the creamed spinach a thicker consistency and prevents the sauce from breaking and becoming oily.

2 tablespoons unsalted butter

1 shallot, minced

2 garlic cloves, minced

1 pound baby spinach, roughly chopped

½ teaspoon kosher salt

½ teaspoon freshly ground black pepper

1 cup heavy (whipping) cream

¼ cup ricotta cheese

¼ cup grated Parmesan cheese

⅛ teaspoon ground nutmeg

1. In a large saucepan, melt the butter over medium heat. Add the shallot and garlic and cook for about 3 minutes, until softened. Add the spinach, a few handfuls at a time, stirring and letting each addition wilt before adding more. Season with the salt and pepper.

2. Stir in the heavy cream and ricotta and cook until the sauce begins to thicken, about 1 minute. Fold in the Parmesan and nutmeg, remove from the heat, and serve.

GARLIC-HERB HASSELBACK POTATOES

Serves 4   Prep time: 15 minutes   Cook time: 50 minutes

These photo-worthy potatoes have parallel slits cut into their tops, making plenty of room for toppings to seep into the crevices of the potato. Cutting slits into the potatoes also speeds up the cooking process and creates crispy edges for added texture. You can make Hasselback potatoes using any type of potato or even another vegetable like zucchini. It's a visually pleasing presentation, not to mention delicious, and is worth the extra few minutes of prep.

2 pounds Yukon Gold or
  red potatoes
2 tablespoons avocado oil
1 teaspoon kosher salt

1 teaspoon freshly ground
  black pepper
4 tablespoons (½ stick)
  unsalted butter
2 garlic cloves, minced

2 tablespoons chopped
  fresh parsley
2 tablespoons grated
  Parmesan cheese

1. Preheat the oven to 425°F.

2. Wash and dry the potatoes and then cut 6 to 8 vertical slits into each one, stopping about three-quarters of the way through (do not cut all the way through the potato).

3. Brush the potatoes with the avocado oil, then season with the salt and pepper. Transfer the potatoes to a baking sheet or cast-iron skillet and bake for 30 minutes, or until the potatoes are golden brown yet slightly undercooked.

4. In a small saucepan over low heat, melt the butter, then stir in the garlic, parsley, and Parmesan cheese. Brush the garlic butter over the potatoes, making sure to get the butter in between the slits. Continue to bake for another 15 to 20 minutes, or until the potatoes are easily pierced with a fork or paring knife.

5. Brush the potatoes with any remaining butter just before serving.

PROSCIUTTO-WRAPPED BRUSSELS SPROUTS

Serves 4   Prep time: 15 minutes   Cook time: 25 minutes

If you hated Brussels sprouts as a kid, you need to give these classed-up sprouts a try. Far from mushy, they are cooked perfectly in the oven and wrapped in salty, crispy prosciutto. There's nothing not to love. When shopping for Brussels sprouts, try to find ones that are sold loosely instead of in a bag so you can pick out the biggest ones. If you can only find the small ones, you can roast the Brussels sprouts separately and crumble the crispy prosciutto over the top.

2 tablespoons olive oil, for greasing

8 to 10 prosciutto slices

1 pound Brussels sprouts, trimmed and halved

½ teaspoon freshly ground black pepper

1 tablespoon balsamic glaze

1 tablespoon grated Parmesan cheese

1. Preheat the oven to 400°F. Grease a baking sheet or large tray with olive oil and set aside.

2. Slice the prosciutto slices crosswise into strips about the same width as the Brussels sprouts. You should get about 3 or 4 strips per slice of prosciutto. Wrap each sprout half in a strip of prosciutto, sprinkle with the pepper, and place cut-side down on the prepared pan.

3. Bake the sprouts for 20 to 25 minutes, or until the prosciutto and the edges of the Brussels sprouts are crispy. Drizzle with the balsamic glaze, top with the Parmesan, and serve.

JALAPEÑO-CHEDDAR MASHED POTATOES

Serves 4   Prep time: 15 minutes   Cook time: 20 minutes

The key to this recipe is bringing some of that good, chargrilled flavor into your potatoes. Since you are already grilling steaks, why not use the grill for your side? Corn and peppers are a classic Southwestern flavor combination that lends itself to some extra smoke. If you don't like spice, you can serve the grilled jalapeño on the side or substitute it with a milder chile such as a poblano or Anaheim (you'll just need one).

1 pound russet potatoes, peeled and cut into chunks

2 corn ears, shucked and rinsed

2 jalapeño peppers

4 tablespoons (½ stick) unsalted butter

1 teaspoon kosher salt

½ teaspoon freshly ground black pepper

¾ cup shredded cheddar cheese

¼ cup sour cream

1. Prepare the grill for direct heat cooking, aiming for a grill temperature of around 400°F

2. Place the potatoes in a medium pot and add enough water to cover them by 1 inch. Bring to a boil over high heat and cook for about 20 minutes, or until the potatoes can be easily pierced with a fork.

3. While the potatoes are boiling, place the corn and jalapeños over direct heat and grill until they are charred on all sides, about 10 minutes. Remove from the heat.

4. Once the corn and peppers have cooled, remove the seeds from the jalapeños and dice the peppers. Shave the corn off the cob and then add the corn and diced jalapeño to a large bowl with the butter.

5. When the potatoes are fork-tender, drain them thoroughly, then add them to the bowl with the corn and jalapeños. Mash the potatoes so the corn and jalapeños are fully incorporated, then season with the salt and pepper and fold in the cheddar and sour cream. Serve immediately.

MUSHROOM RISOTTO

Serves 4   Prep time: 10 minutes   Cook time: 40 minutes

It always amazes me how creamy risotto is without having any actual milk or cream in it. The natural starches in the rice release and not only thicken the risotto but also create that velvety smooth texture that is associated with this classic rice dish. As a result, risotto is rich and flavorful without being heavy, making it a great accompaniment for steak. I use beef stock and red wine if I make this recipe with beef, but I will use chicken stock and white wine if I'm serving it with fish, pork, or chicken.

8 cups beef stock

1 cup red wine

2 tablespoons Worcestershire sauce

2 bay leaves

1 teaspoon chopped fresh thyme

2 tablespoons unsalted butter

4 garlic cloves, minced

½ cup chopped scallions, both white and green parts, divided

2 cups sliced button mushrooms

2 cups arborio rice

1 cup frozen peas

½ cup grated Parmesan cheese

2 tablespoons chopped fresh parsley

Kosher salt

Freshly ground black pepper

1. In a 4-quart pot, bring the beef stock, wine, Worcestershire sauce, bay leaves, and thyme to a simmer over medium-high heat.

2. In a large Dutch oven or large pot over medium heat, melt the butter. Add the garlic and white parts of the scallions and sauté for about 2 minutes, until soft. Add the mushrooms and cook for about 3 minutes, until slightly tender.

3. Add the arborio rice and cook, stirring, to lightly toast the rice, 2 to 3 minutes. Add the stock mixture, without the bay leaves, 1 cup at a time, letting most of the liquid absorb into the rice before adding more. There should be just enough stock to completely cover the rice. Stir, adding the stock while cooking for 15 to 20 minutes, until all the stock has been incorporated into the rice.

4. Add the frozen peas and continue to stir until the rice is fully cooked and tender.

5. Fold in the Parmesan cheese, parsley, and green parts of the scallions. Season with salt and pepper and serve.

ROSEMARY-TRUFFLE FRIES

Serves 4 Prep time: 15 minutes, plus 3 hours or overnight to soak
Cook time: 10 minutes, plus 30 minutes or 4 hours to rest

Truffles and potatoes have always been one of my favorite flavor combinations because of the way the robust, earthy flavor of the truffle blends harmoniously with the potatoes. Truffle oil can be a splurge, but it's worth it. It's a versatile pantry ingredient that can be drizzled over meats and vegetables for special occasions. The key to perfect fries (or frites) is cooking the potatoes twice. This will remove moisture and give you extra-crispy fries to serve alongside a steak. I also recommend a sauce or compound butter to dip the frites and steak in.

2 tablespoons white vinegar
6 to 8 cups water
4 large russet potatoes, peeled
8 cups canola oil

2 rosemary sprigs
2 teaspoons truffle oil (optional)
1 teaspoon sea salt

¼ teaspoon freshly ground
    black pepper
2 tablespoons freshly shaved
    Parmesan cheese

1. In a medium bowl, combine the vinegar with the water. Cut the potatoes lengthwise into ¼-inch-thick slices, then cut the slices crosswise into long ¼-inch-thick frites. Transfer the frites to the prepared vinegar solution, topping the potatoes with a plate to keep them submerged. Let soak for at least 3 hours or as long as overnight.

2. Line a baking sheet or large tray with paper towels. Drain the potatoes and pat them dry. In a 4-quart Dutch oven or a tabletop fryer, heat the canola oil to 275°F.

3. Working in batches, fry the potatoes for 3 to 5 minutes, until slightly softened. Do not brown the potatoes during this step. Transfer the potatoes to the paper towel–lined baking sheet and let cool for at least 30 minutes, or up to 4 hours.

4. Raise the temperature of the oil to 350°F. Carefully place the blanched frites into the oil and cook for 3 to 5 minutes, or until golden and crispy. Just before the frites are golden, place a sprig of fresh rosemary in the oil for the final minute of the cooking process. Watch out for popping oil.

5. Transfer the frites to a bowl and toss with the truffle oil (if using), salt, and pepper. Crumble the crispy rosemary over the frites and top with the Parmesan cheese before serving hot.

GRILLED CAESAR SALAD

Serves 4   Prep time: 15 minutes, plus 30 minutes to refrigerate   Cook time: 5 minutes

This warm dish is a fun take on the classic Caesar salad and an easy side that is great with just about any cut of beef. A shortcut homemade Caesar dressing (made with mayonnaise, so you don't have to worry about raw eggs) gets brushed onto halved romaine hearts before grilling just long enough to give the lettuce a delicious char without wilting it too much. I also add halved cherry tomatoes, which add color and freshness to the dish and amplify an already beautiful presentation.

For the dressing

¾ cup mayonnaise

½ cup grated Parmesan cheese

4 garlic cloves, minced

4 anchovy fillets or 2 teaspoons anchovy paste

Juice of 2 lemons

2 tablespoons olive oil

1 tablespoon Dijon mustard

1 tablespoon Worcestershire sauce

½ teaspoon freshly ground black pepper

2 tablespoons water, as needed

4 romaine hearts

¼ cup shredded Parmesan cheese

1 cup croutons

1 cup cherry tomatoes, halved

1. **To make the dressing:** In a small bowl, whisk together the mayonnaise, Parmesan, garlic, anchovy, lemon juice, olive oil, Dijon mustard, Worcestershire sauce, and pepper until smooth. If preferred, make a smoother dressing in a blender. If the dressing is too thick, you can thin it out with a few tablespoons of water. Refrigerate for 30 minutes.

2. Prepare the grill for direct-heat grilling, aiming for a grill temperature of 400°F to 450°F.

3. Remove any damaged leaves from the lettuce and then split each romaine heart down the center with a knife, leaving the stem attached.

4. Brush the cut side of each half of romaine with about 2 tablespoons of dressing, then place the romaine cut-side down on the grill. Sear the romaine for about 90 seconds, just until you have a slight char, then immediately remove it from the grill onto a platter.

5. Drizzle additional dressing over the lettuce, then top with the shredded Parmesan, croutons, and tomatoes and serve.

GRILLED LEMON-PEPPER BROCCOLI

Serves 4   Prep time: 5 minutes   Cook time: 15 minutes

This simple side dish is great when you don't want something heavy. The bright citrus accentuates the broccoli nicely without overpowering the veggies. As the broccoli grills, the florets get crispy and the stems become tender and, believe it or not, slightly sweet. You can serve grilled broccoli with literally any cut or type of cuisine, so it's a perfect dish to have in your toolbox.

2 broccoli crowns, cut into florets

2 tablespoons avocado oil

1 teaspoon kosher salt

1 teaspoon lemon-pepper seasoning

2 tablespoons unsalted butter, melted

2 tablespoons freshly squeezed lemon juice

1. In a large bowl, toss the broccoli with the avocado oil, salt, and lemon-pepper seasoning.

2. Prepare the grill for dual-zone cooking with the coals off to one side. Aim for a grill temperature of 350°F to 400°F.

3. Place the broccoli spears on the grill over direct heat and cook for about 2 minutes before turning. Once the broccoli is grilled on both sides, continue to turn every minute or so until it is charred on the outside and slightly tender, 8 to 10 minutes.

4. If the broccoli still isn't tender, move it to indirect heat and continue to cook until tender.

5. Remove the broccoli from the grill and finish with a drizzle of melted butter and lemon juice.

CLASSIC MAC AND CHEESE

Serves 4   Prep time: 20 minutes   Cook time: 45 minutes

Whether you're making it for a kid or a kid at heart, mac and cheese is always a hit. The cheesy, melty goodness with a kiss of heat from the grill makes this a favorite side dish for any steak dinner. You can serve this recipe family-style or in smaller individual containers. The panko bread crumbs on top absorb the sauce and give the creamy mac and cheese a little crunch.

8 ounces elbow macaroni, cooked

2½ cups shredded sharp cheddar cheese, divided

8 ounces Velveeta cheese, cubed

½ cup heavy (whipping) cream

½ teaspoon kosher salt

½ teaspoon freshly ground black pepper

2 tablespoons unsalted butter, for greasing

1 cup panko bread crumbs

2 tablespoons chopped fresh parsley

1. Set up the grill for indirect heat with all the coals pushed to one side. Aim for a grill temperature of 350°F to 400°F.

2. In a large bowl, mix together the cooked pasta with 2 cups of cheddar cheese, the Velveeta, heavy cream, salt, and pepper. Transfer to a large cast-iron skillet or oven-safe casserole dish greased with the butter. Spread the mac and cheese mixture out evenly.

3. Place the skillet on the indirect side of the grill and cook for 30 minutes. Once all the cheese is melted, stir the mixture until smooth, then top with the bread crumbs and remaining ½ cup of cheddar.

4. Bake for 10 to 15 minutes more, until bubbling. Remove the mac and cheese from the grill and garnish with fresh chopped parsley. Let it rest for 5 to 10 minutes before serving.

STEAK HOUSE ONION RINGS

Serves 4   Prep time: 15 minutes   Cook time: 5 minutes per batch

Crispy onion rings with a big juicy steak is the epitome of a classic steak house dish. This recipe can be prepared in a Dutch oven or a tabletop fryer for ultimate crispiness. If you don't want to set up the fryer, you can also make a slightly healthier version using an oven or air fryer. The onion rings will be a little less crispy but still very tasty. When you are shopping for onions, be sure to select large onions without any dents or bruises.

For the dry dredge

¾ cup all-purpose flour
¼ cup cornstarch
1 teaspoon kosher salt
1 teaspoon freshly ground
   black pepper
1 teaspoon smoked paprika

For the wet dredge

¾ cup heavy (whipping) cream
2 large eggs
1 teaspoon freshly ground
   black pepper
1 teaspoon kosher salt

2 cups panko bread crumbs
8 cups canola oil, for frying
4 large onions, cut into ½-inch-
   thick rings, separated

1. **To make the dry dredge:** In a medium bowl, combine the flour, cornstarch, salt, pepper, and paprika.

2. **To make the wet dredge:** In another medium bowl, combine the cream, eggs, pepper, and salt.

3. In another medium bowl, pour in the bread crumbs.

4. Pour the oil into a Dutch oven or tabletop fryer and preheat to 350°F or preheat the oven or air fryer to 400°F.

5. Coat each onion ring in the dry dredge, then the wet dredge, and then the panko bread crumbs. Make sure to pack the bread crumbs into each onion ring to help them stick. Repeat the process for all the onion rings.

6. To fry, carefully place each onion ring into the hot oil and cook, in batches, for 3 to 5 minutes, or until the onion rings are floating in the oil and golden brown. For the oven method, lightly spray each onion ring with cooking oil, then place the onion rings on a sheet pan and bake for 12 to 15 minutes, or until golden and crispy.

5

RUBS and SAUCES

At the end of the day, you can make a great steak with just salt, pepper, and a good quality piece of meat. However, that doesn't mean that you can't also enhance those flavors with sauces and rubs that take things to another level. Subtle flavors from herbs and spices can take an average steak and make it great without ruining the integrity of the meat. Sauces and marinades can also elevate a cheaper cut of meat, making it taste like a much more expensive cut. These are just a few of my favorite rubs and sauces that can lend a hand when you're looking to add flavor to your steak.

Compound Butter 100

Homemade Steak Sauce 102

Espresso Rub 103

Dijon Cream Sauce 104

Stout Pan Sauce 105

Blender Hollandaise Sauce 106

Worcestershire Steak Marinade 107

COMPOUND BUTTER

Serves 4   Prep time: 15 minutes   Cook time: 5 minutes

When it comes to adding rich, buttery flavor to steaks, compound butter is your best friend. You can create so many different flavor profiles, from bold and spicy to herbaceous and even sweet. The key to making compound butter is to make sure the butter is entirely soft—but not melted—before adding the flavorings or mix-ins. Here are just a few of my favorite combinations that you can make easily at home.

Garlic-Herb Compound Butter

8 tablespoons (1 stick) unsalted butter,
    at room temperature
2 garlic cloves, minced
1½ teaspoons chopped fresh parsley
1 teaspoon chopped fresh rosemary
1 teaspoon chopped fresh thyme
½ teaspoon red pepper flakes
¼ teaspoon sea salt
¼ teaspoon freshly ground black pepper

Ginger-Soy Compound Butter

8 tablespoons (1 stick) unsalted butter,
    at room temperature
2 garlic cloves, minced
1 tablespoon chopped fresh cilantro
1 tablespoon thinly sliced scallions, both
    white and green parts
1½ teaspoons soy sauce
1½ teaspoons sriracha
1½ teaspoons black and/or white
    sesame seeds (optional)
1 teaspoon minced fresh ginger

Bacon and Blue Cheese Compound Butter

8 tablespoons (1 stick) unsalted butter,
    at room temperature
2 tablespoons chopped crispy
    cooked bacon
2 tablespoons crumbled blue cheese
1½ teaspoons chopped fresh parsley
¼ teaspoon sea salt
¼ teaspoon freshly ground black pepper

Horseradish Compound Butter

8 tablespoons (1 stick) unsalted butter,
    at room temperature
1 tablespoon prepared horseradish
1 tablespoon thinly sliced scallions, both
    white and green parts
1½ teaspoons Worcestershire sauce
½ teaspoon freshly ground black pepper
¼ teaspoon sea salt

Shallot Compound Butter

8 tablespoons (1 stick) unsalted butter,
    at room temperature
½ cup minced shallots
1 garlic clove, chopped
1½ teaspoons Worcestershire sauce
1½ teaspoons thinly sliced scallions,
    both white and green parts
½ teaspoon chopped fresh thyme
½ teaspoon freshly ground black pepper
¼ teaspoon sea salt

1. In a stand mixer with a paddle attachment or in a large bowl using a spatula, combine the butter with the other ingredients.

2. Once the ingredients are well incorporated, place the butter in the center of a sheet of parchment paper. Fold the paper over the butter and mold it into a cylinder shape. Roll the log of butter up completely and fold in the sides of the parchment paper. Then wrap it in plastic wrap or place it in a large resealable plastic bag.

3. Store for up to 1 month in the refrigerator or up to 6 months in the freezer.

4. To serve, cut a ¼-inch-thick slice of the butter and place it on a warm steak to melt.

Perfect Partner: **This compound butter is a great way to add flavor and fat to a lean steak like a filet mignon or a top sirloin.**

HOMEMADE STEAK SAUCE

Makes 3 cups   Prep time: 15 minutes   Cook time: 20 minutes

Some steak purists will say that if you put steak sauce on a steak, you're just covering up the flavor of the steak. I argue that this steak sauce can enhance the taste of the meat without disguising it. This sauce can be made at home, and I believe it is a fantastic condiment to serve at your next cookout. Making your own steak sauce is also a great flex. When someone asks if you have A.1. steak sauce, you can tell them you have something even better!

1 cup water
½ onion, roughly chopped
¼ cup balsamic vinegar
¼ cup Worcestershire sauce
¼ cup raisins
Juice of 1 orange

2 tablespoons soy sauce
2 garlic cloves, peeled
   and smashed
2 tablespoons whole
   peppercorns

1 cup ketchup
1 teaspoon mustard powder
1 tablespoon smoked paprika
1 tablespoon hot sauce

1. In a small saucepan over medium-low heat, combine the water, onion, vinegar, Worcestershire sauce, raisins, orange juice, soy sauce, garlic, and peppercorns. Simmer for about 20 minutes, but do not let the liquid come to a rolling boil.

2. Strain the liquid into a bowl and let it cool for 10 minutes, then whisk in the ketchup, mustard powder, paprika, and hot sauce. Store in an airtight container in the refrigerator for up to 2 months.

ESPRESSO RUB

Makes ½ cup   Prep time: 5 minutes

For all my coffee lovers out there, this rub is for you. Espresso gives a distinct earthy flavor to steaks and creates an unbelievable crust. You can store this rub in a mason jar and have it on hand anytime the mood hits you to grill. Even if you don't drink coffee, I bet that the roasted flavor of the coffee combined with the smoky chipotle powder will have you hooked.

2 tablespoons coarsely ground espresso

1 tablespoon kosher salt

1 tablespoon freshly ground black pepper

1 tablespoon smoked paprika

1 tablespoon chipotle powder

1 tablespoon brown sugar

1 teaspoon granulated garlic

1 teaspoon granulated onion

1. In a small bowl, combine the espresso, salt, pepper, paprika, chipotle powder, brown sugar, granulated garlic, and granulated onion, breaking up any clumps.

2. Transfer to an airtight container and store for up to 4 months in a cool, dry place out of direct sunlight.

DIJON CREAM SAUCE

Makes ¾ cup   Prep time: 5 minutes   Cook time: 10 minutes

Whenever I need a last-minute sauce, this is the recipe I make. It can be cooked in less than 10 minutes and uses ingredients you probably have on hand already. All of the components work well together, giving this sauce a tangy yet rich flavor that's great for any cut of steak. This sauce is also fantastic drizzled over grilled veggies like asparagus and broccoli.

2 tablespoons unsalted butter

2 garlic cloves, minced

1 shallot, minced, or ¼ red onion, diced

¼ cup white wine

2 tablespoons Dijon mustard

½ cup heavy (whipping) cream

2 tablespoons thinly sliced chives

Kosher salt

Freshly ground black pepper

1. In a medium sauté pan over medium heat, melt the butter. Add the garlic and shallots and cook for about 1 minute, until softened, then add the white wine and Dijon mustard. Cook for 1 minute more, stirring to combine, then cook until the sauce has reduced by half, about 2 minutes.

2. Pour in the heavy cream and cook until the sauce again reduces by half and coats the back of a spoon, 1 to 2 minutes.

3. Taste and add salt and pepper as needed. Add the chives just before serving.

STOUT PAN SAUCE

Makes 1 cup   Prep time: 15 minutes   Cook time: 5 minutes

If you love dark Irish stouts, I highly recommend you make this quick and easy pan sauce. I find that this sauce is best if you make it when searing steak tips in a pan, so that you can make the sauce in the same pan and pick up the flavors of the steak. You can also prepare this sauce on its own and drizzle it over any cut of beef. It reminds me of a gravy but with a deeper, bolder flavor.

1 tablespoon unsalted butter
1 shallot, minced
2 garlic cloves, minced
½ cup beef broth

½ cup stout beer, such
    as Guinness
1 tablespoon
    Worcestershire sauce
2 tablespoons sour cream

½ teaspoon freshly ground
    black pepper
1 tablespoon thinly sliced
    scallions, both white and
    green parts

1. In a medium skillet over medium heat, melt the butter and sauté the shallots and garlic for about 1 minute, just until soft. Deglaze the pan with the beef broth, stout beer, and Worcestershire sauce, scraping up any browned bits, and simmer until reduced by half, 3 to 4 minutes. Then reduce the heat to low and whisk in the sour cream.

2. Add the pepper and scallions. If the sauce seems too thin, whisk in an additional 1 tablespoon of sour cream.

BLENDER HOLLANDAISE SAUCE

Makes about ¾ cup   Prep time: 5 minutes   Cook time: 5 minutes

Hollandaise is a classic French sauce and one of the most magical things you will ever taste. Emulsified butter and egg yolks with a hint of lemon and hot sauce make a silky-smooth sauce that is often served with eggs Benedict or poured over steaks and vegetables. This blender version takes all the hard work of whisking out of the equation, and in a few minutes you will have this rich, buttery goodness at the ready.

8 tablespoons (1 stick) unsalted butter

3 large egg yolks

1 tablespoon freshly squeezed lemon juice

½ teaspoon kosher salt

1 teaspoon Tabasco sauce or other hot sauce

¼ teaspoon ground white pepper (optional)

1. Place the butter in a microwave-safe bowl and microwave for 30 to 45 seconds to melt.

2. In a blender, combine the egg yolks and lemon juice and blend for about 30 seconds, until the color of the yolks becomes lighter.

3. Through the opening at the top of the blender, begin pouring the butter very slowly into the blender until the sauce becomes thick and coats the back of a spoon.

4. Add the salt, Tabasco, and white pepper (if using) and pulse to incorporate. If the sauce is too thick, add 1 tablespoon of warm water and pulse until smooth and thinned out.

Tip: Hollandaise cannot be reheated, but it can be stored in an insulated thermos or coffee mug for a few hours, and it will stay warm.

WORCESTERSHIRE STEAK MARINADE

Makes 1¼ cups   Prep time: 10 minutes

This is a workhorse, all-purpose marinade that can be adjusted to your taste. It is my go-to marinade when I want to add a blast of flavor to steaks or roasts. If you like a spicier kick, feel free to add chopped jalapeño, cayenne powder, or even your favorite hot sauce. You can also add ingredients like ginger or cilantro to change up the flavor profile to fit the type of cuisine you're making.

¾ cup olive oil

½ cup chopped yellow onion

3 tablespoons Worcestershire sauce

Juice of 1 lemon

2 tablespoons Dijon mustard

2 tablespoons chopped fresh parsley

1 tablespoon white vinegar

4 garlic cloves, minced

2 teaspoons freshly ground black pepper

1 teaspoon sea salt

1. In a blender or food processor, combine the olive oil, onion, Worcestershire sauce, lemon juice, Dijon mustard, parsley, vinegar, garlic, pepper, and salt. Pulse for a few seconds at a time, just long enough to incorporate the ingredients but still leave some chunks.

2. Pour the marinade over the meat and marinate for up to 24 hours. Marinade should be discarded once used with raw meat, but unused marinade can be stored for up to 7 days in an airtight container in the refrigerator.

MEASUREMENT CONVERSIONS

	US STANDARD	US STANDARD (ounces)	METRIC (approximate)
VOLUME EQUIVALENTS (Liquid)	2 tablespoons	1 fl. oz.	30 mL
	¼ cup	2 fl. oz.	60 mL
	½ cup	4 fl. oz.	120 mL
	1 cup	8 fl. oz.	240 mL
	1½ cups	12 fl. oz.	355 mL
	2 cups or 1 pint	16 fl. oz.	475 mL
	4 cups or 1 quart	32 fl. oz.	1 L
	1 gallon	128 fl. oz.	4 L
VOLUME EQUIVALENTS (Dry)	⅛ teaspoon		0.5 mL
	¼ teaspoon		1 mL
	½ teaspoon		2 mL
	¾ teaspoon		4 mL
	1 teaspoon		5 mL
	1 tablespoon		15 mL
	¼ cup		59 mL
	⅓ cup		79 mL
	½ cup		118 mL
	⅔ cup		156 mL
	¾ cup		177 mL
	1 cup		235 mL
	2 cups or 1 pint		475 mL
	3 cups		700 mL
	4 cups or 1 quart		1 L
	½ gallon		2 L
	1 gallon		4 L
WEIGHT EQUIVALENTS	½ ounce		15 g
	1 ounce		30 g
	2 ounces		60 g
	4 ounces		115 g
	8 ounces		225 g
	12 ounces		340 g
	16 ounces or 1 pound		455 g

	FAHRENHEIT (F)	CELSIUS (C) (APPROXIMATE)
OVEN TEMPERATURES	250°F	120°C
	300°F	150°C
	325°F	180°C
	375°F	190°C
	400°F	200°C
	425°F	220°C
	450°F	230°C

INDEX

═══

A

all natural beef, 7
Angus beef, 6

B

béarnaise sauce, 44
beef
    aging techniques and
       tenderness, 4
    buying guide, 5
    cuts of, 2
    diet of the bovine, 3–4
    flavor of, 3–4
    grading levels, 6
    know your butcher, 5
    shopping for, 7
    tenderness of, 2–3
beer/stout
    Guinness, 105
black and blue, 26, 51
Black Angus, 6
bone-in
    prime rib, 46
    rib eye steaks, 16, 36, 40, 52, 57

C

Caesar dressing, 94
certified organic beef, 6
choice beef, 6
chuck steak. *See* Denver Steak
crabmeat, 44

D

Denver steak (chuck)
    Denver Steak with Horseradish
      Sauce, 69
    know your steaks, 12
Dutch oven, 97

F

filet mignon/beef tenderloin
    Blue Cheese and Bacon
      Carpetbagger, 51
    know your steaks, 8
    no need to marinate, 19
    Pastrami-Crusted Beef
      Tenderloin, 66–67
    selecting the right steak, 4
flank steak
    Bavette with Burgundy Sauce, 56
    French Onion Steak, 73
    know your steaks, 10
    marinade, 21
    Steak Caprese, 63
    Steak Fajitas, 38–39
flat iron steak
    Flat Iron Steak with Tarragon
      Sauce, 68
    Grilled Steak Oscar, 44–45
    know your steaks, 13

G

grass-fed beef, 3, 4, 6
gravy
    mushroom, 42

grilling

grilling
    blot it dry, 22
    doneness level, 25–26
    grilling tools, 18–19
    let it rest, 27
    reverse sear, 24
    slicing your steaks, 27
    thick steaks, 23
    thinner steaks, 25
grills
    charcoal, 15, 16, 17, 18–19, 23, 25
    direct fire, 15
    gas, 15–16, 17, 18, 23, 25
    grilling techniques, 19–20,
      23, 24, 26
    how to choose the right, 1, 15–16
    indirect fire, 17
    sear temperature, 17–18

H

hanger steak
    know your steaks, 12
    Steak Benedict, 80–81
    Steak Marsala, 36–37
    Thai Beef Salad, 50
hollandaise sauce, 44, 106

I

injections, 21
Irish stouts, 105
Italian cuisine, 48, 63
Italian seasoning, 56, 63, 84

J

Jaccard/meat mallet, 22

M

marinade
　fajita, 38
　flavor enhancer, 14, 22
　hoisin/soy sauce, 70
　over-marinating, 21
　pineapple and soy, 76
　remove the excess, 21–22
　sweet and salty, 32
　tenderize any cut, 6, 20–21, 22, 99
　use with brine, 22
　Worcestershire Steak
　　Marinade, 107
measurement conversion chart, 108

P

perfect partner, 28
picanha
　Picanha with Chimichurri, 54–55
porterhouse/T-bone
　Bistecca Fiorentina, 48–49
　choosing the best steak, 4
　know your steaks, 9
　place directly on coals, 16
　South African Braai-Spiced
　　Steak, 52–53
prime beef, 6
prime rib
　know your steaks, 8
　Rosemary-Crusted Prime
　　Rib, 46–47, **x**

R

rib eye steak
　best way to cook, 8, 19
　Blackened Rib Eye with Cajun
　　Cream Sauce, 62
　Bourbon-Butter Tomahawk Rib
　　Eye, 64–65
　buttery flavor, 3
　Eisenhower Cowboy
　　Rib Eye, 40–41

non-weight bearing cut, 2
　Philly Steak Rib Eye, 72
round steak
　affordable cut, 2
　know your steaks, 13
　marinade, 20
　Pineapple and Soy Sauce–
　　Marinated Round
　　Steaks, 76–77
　Salisbury Steak, 42–43
Rubs and Sauces
　Blender Hollandaise
　　Sauce, 106
　Compound Butters, 100–101
　Dijon Cream Sauce, 104
　Espresso Rub, 103
　Homemade Steak Sauce, 102
　Stout Pan Sauce, 105
　Worcestershire Steak
　　Marinade, 107

S

Salisbury, James, 42
sauce
　Burgundy sauce, 56
　Cajun cream sauce, 62
　horseradish sauce, 69
　tarragon, 68
select beef, 6
short ribs
　know your steaks, 14
　Korean Kalbi, 32–33
sirloin/top sirloin steak
　Hoisin-Glazed Sirloin
　　Skewers, 70–71
　know your steaks, 10
　Steak Chesapeake, 60–61
skirt steak
　Jalapeño-Popper
　　Pinwheels, 78–79
　know your steaks, 11
　marinating, 20
　Steak Fajitas, 38–39
Steak Classics
　Bavette with Burgundy Sauce, 56
　Bistecca Fiorentina, 48–49

Blue Cheese and Bacon
　Carpetbagger, 51
Eisenhower Cowboy
　Rib Eye, 40–41
Grilled Steak Oscar, 44–45
Grilled Strip Steak with Charred
　Tomatoes, 57, **viii**
Korean Kalbi, 32–33
Picanha with Chimichurri, 54–55
Rosemary-Crusted prime
　Rib, 46–47, **x**
Salisbury Steak, 42–43
South African Braai-Spiced
　Steak, 52–53
Steak au Poivre, 34–35
Steak Fajitas, **30,** 38–39
Steak marsala, 36–37
Thai Beef Salad, 50
steak cuts
　porterhouse, 48
Steak House Sides
　Classic Mac and Cheese, 96
　Creamed Spinach, **86,** 88
　Garlic-Herb Hasselback
　　Potatoes, 89
　Grilled Caesar Salad, 94
　Grilled Lemon-Pepper
　　Broccoli, 95
　Jalapéno-Cheddar Mashed
　　Potatoes, 91
　Mushroom Risotto, 92
　Prosciutto-Wrapped Brussels
　　Sprouts, 90
　Rosemary-Truffle Fries, 93
　Steak House Onion Rings, 97
steak swap
　boneless roast, 47, 75
　filet mignon/hanger
　　steak, 35, 45, 61, 62, 63,
　　67, 81, 85
　ground beef patties, 43
　London broil, 33
　porterhouse, 41, 49, 52
　rib eye, 52, 57, 65
　sirloin/baseball steak, 51, 83
　strip steak/Denver/flank, 37, 39,
　　50, 56, 68, 69, 71, 77, 79
　tri tip, 54

Steak Unleashed
    Blackened Rib Eye with Cajun
       Cream Sauce, 62
    Bourbon-Butter Tomahawk Rib
       Eye, 64–65
    Country Fried Steak with Black
       Pepper Gravy, 82–83
    Denver Steak with Horseradish
       Sauce, 69
    Flat Iron Steak with Tarragon
       Sauce, 68
    French Onion Steak, 73
    Hoisin-Glazed Sirloin
       Skewers, **58,** 70–71
    Jalapeño-Popper
       Pinwheels, 78–79
    Jerk-Marinated Tri-Tip, 74–75
    Pastrami-Crusted Beef
       Tenderloin, 66–67
    Philly Steak Rib Eye, 72

    Pineapple and Soy Sauce–
       Marinated Round
       Steaks, 76–77
    Steak and Shrimp Scampi, 84–85
    Steak Benedict, 80–81
    Steak Caprese, 63
    Steak Chesapeake, 60–61
strip steak
    Grilled Strip Steak with Charred
       Tomatoes, 57, **viii**
    know your steaks, 9
    Steak and Shrimp Scampi, 84–85
    Steak au Poivre, 34–35
    tenderness of, 2–3, 19

T
Tabasco sauce, 44
tri tip
    Jerk-Marinated Tri Tip, 74–75

    know your steaks, 14
    marinade/injections, 21
    tenderness of, 3
TV dinners, 42

U
USDA shield, 6

V
variation tip, 28
veal cutlets, 44

W
Wagyu/Kobe beef, 3, 6

ABOUT THE AUTHOR

 Frank Campanella is the owner of the popular food blogs Grilling24x7.com and CulinaryLion.com. Frank has been an award-winning chef and post-master at numerous restaurants in the mid-Atlantic region, and has also has won multiple awards with his Kansas City Barbecue Society competition team, Godfather BBQ.

CPSIA information can be obtained
at www.ICGtesting.com
Printed in the USA
JSHW011015190422
24993JS00003B/3